I0507828

THIS BOOK

belongs to

....

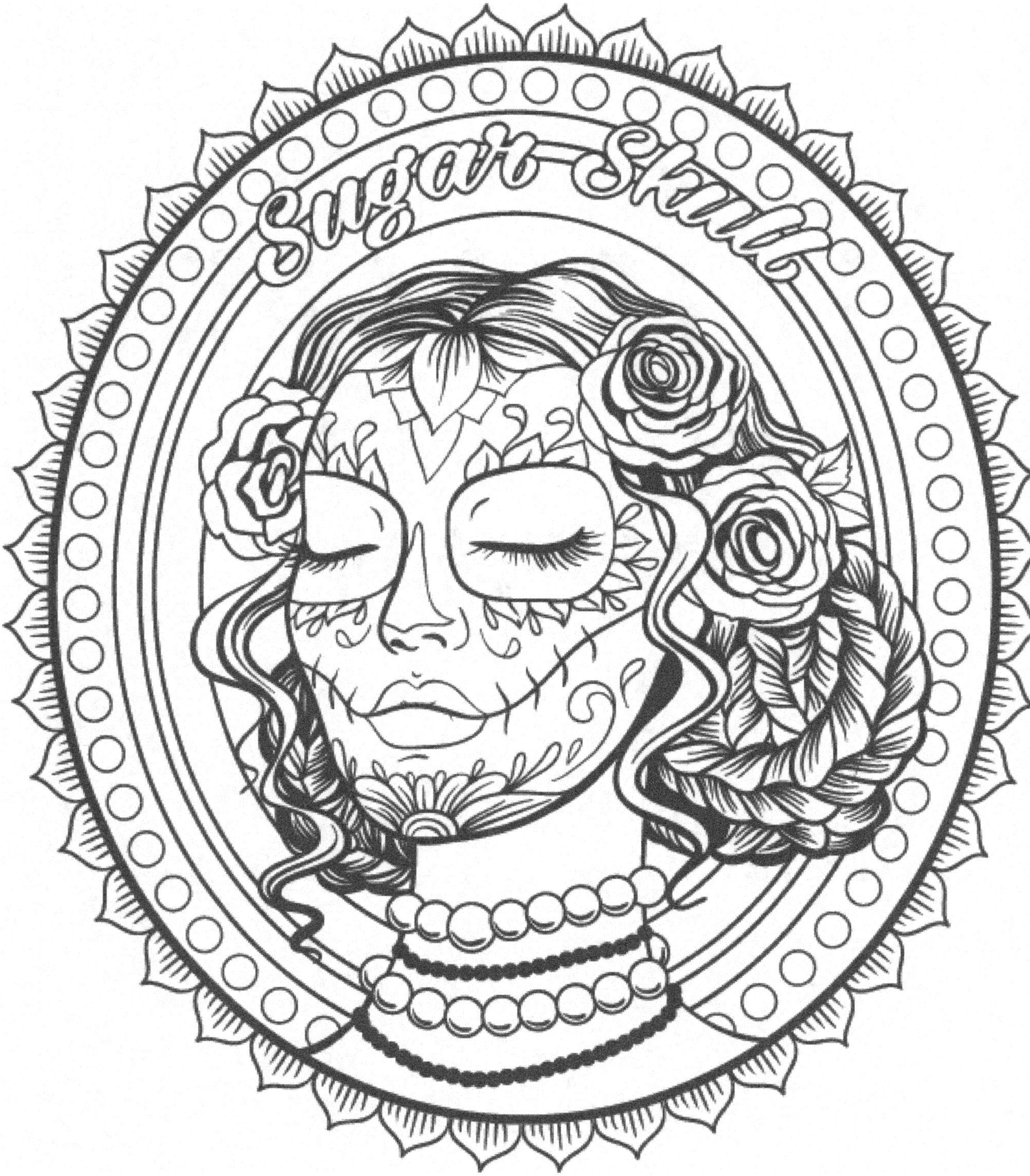
Sugar Skull

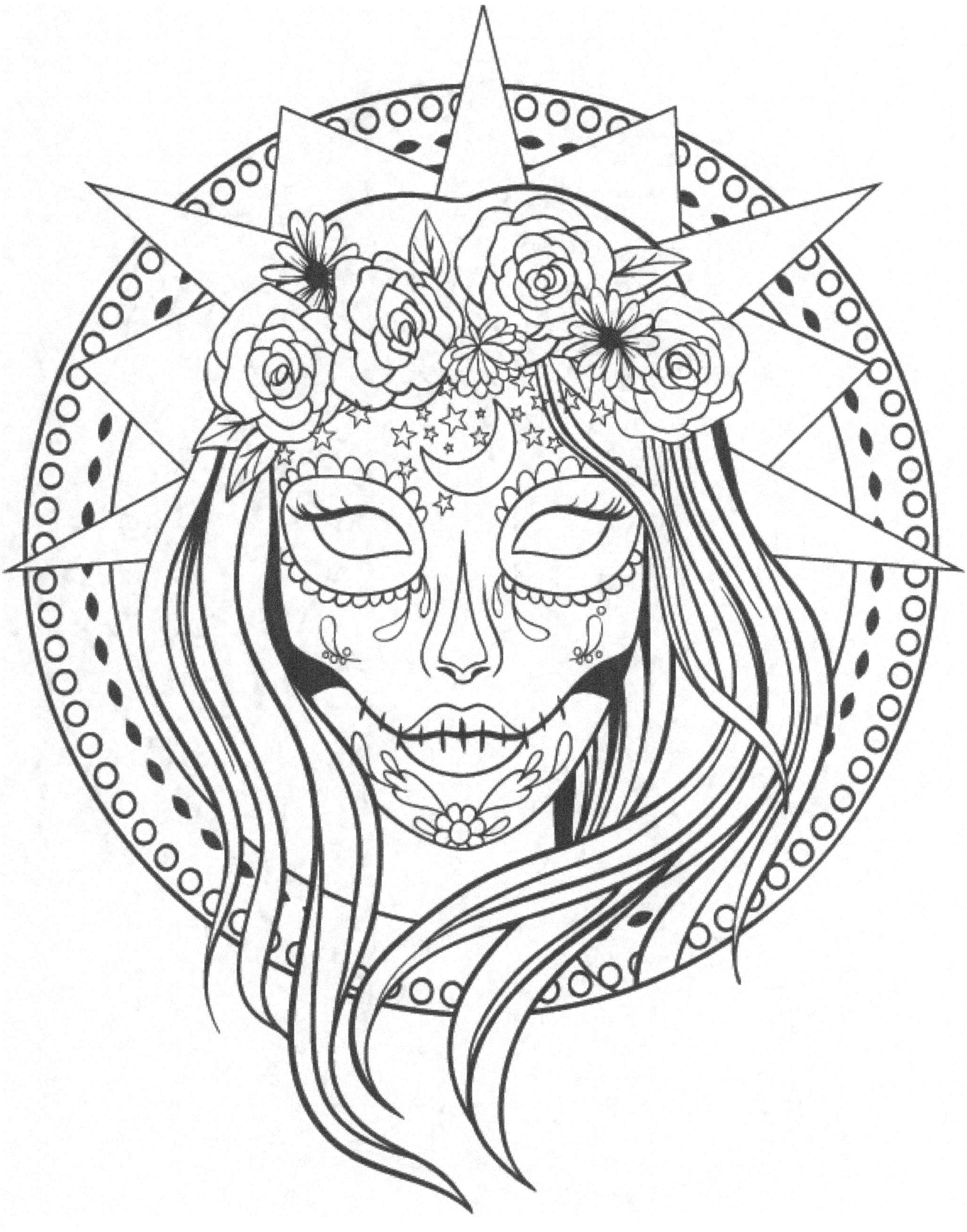

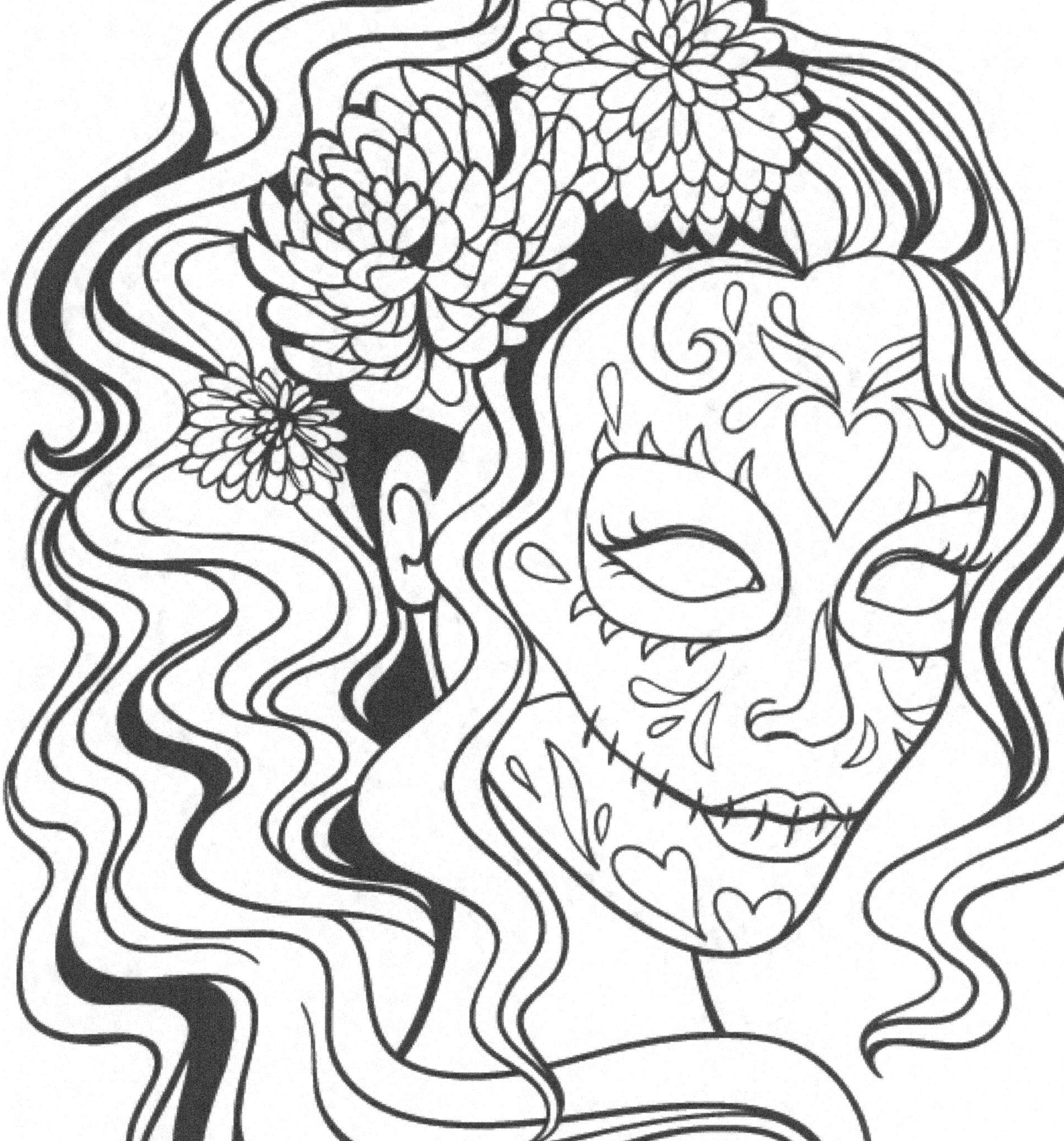

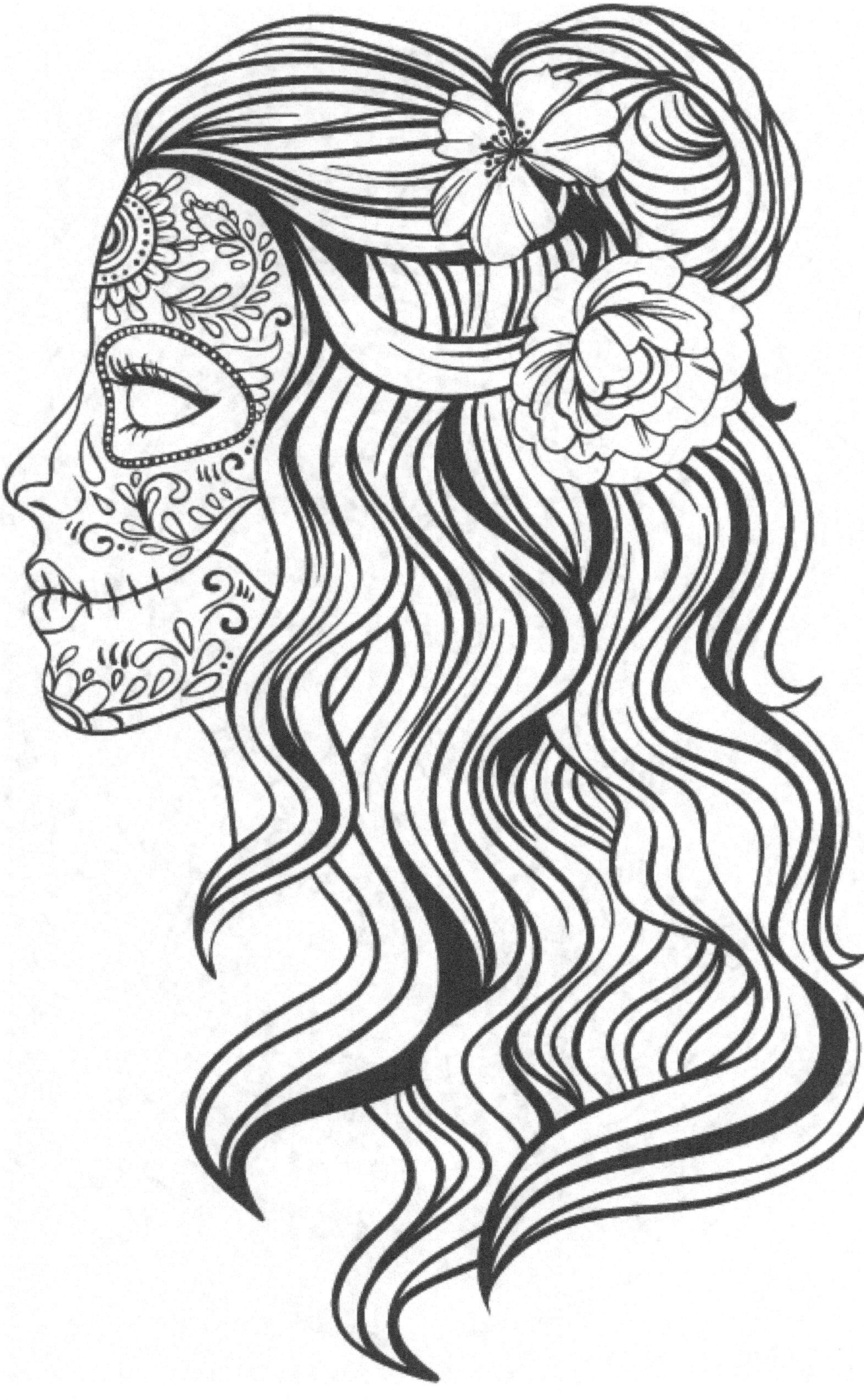

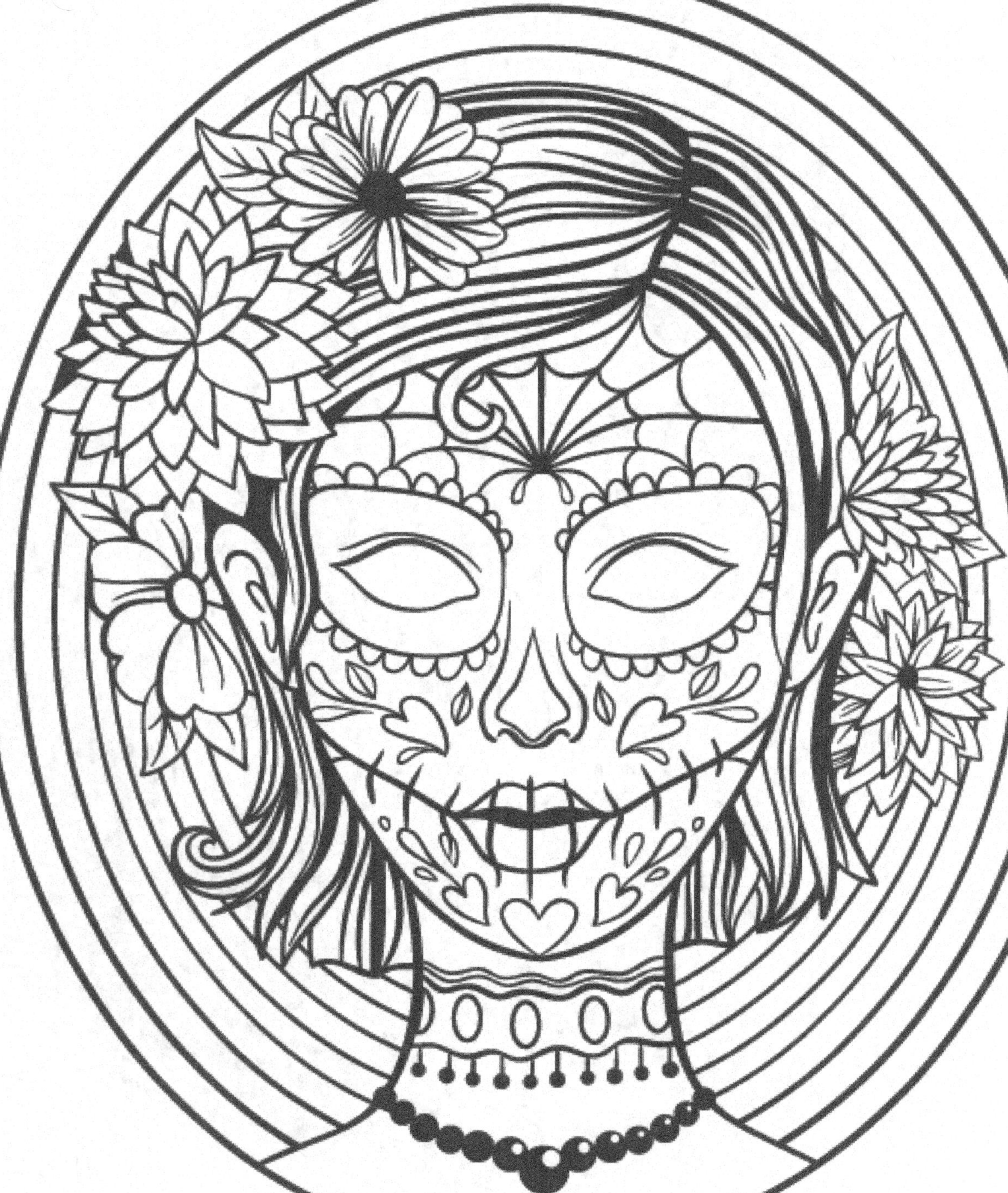

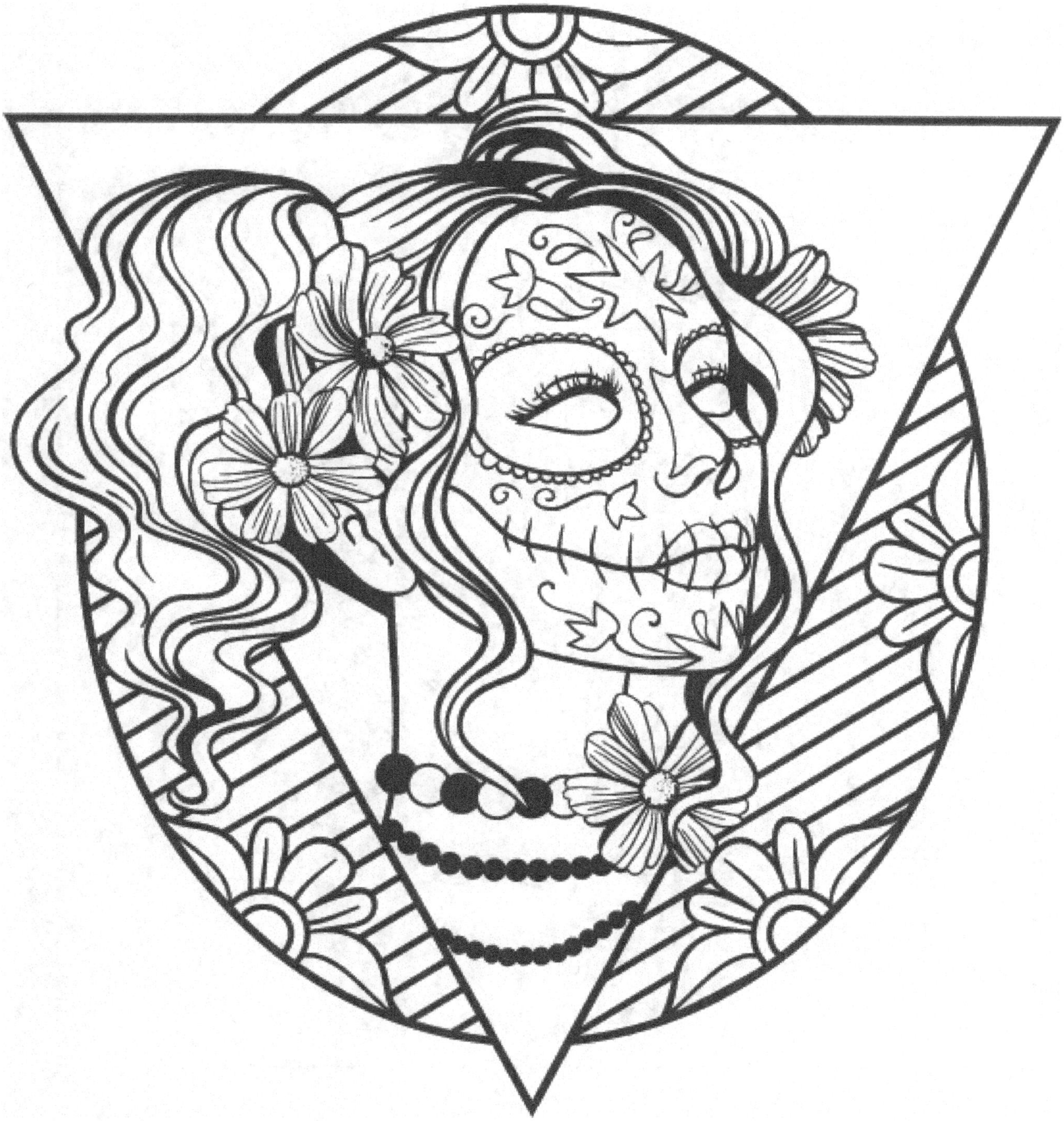

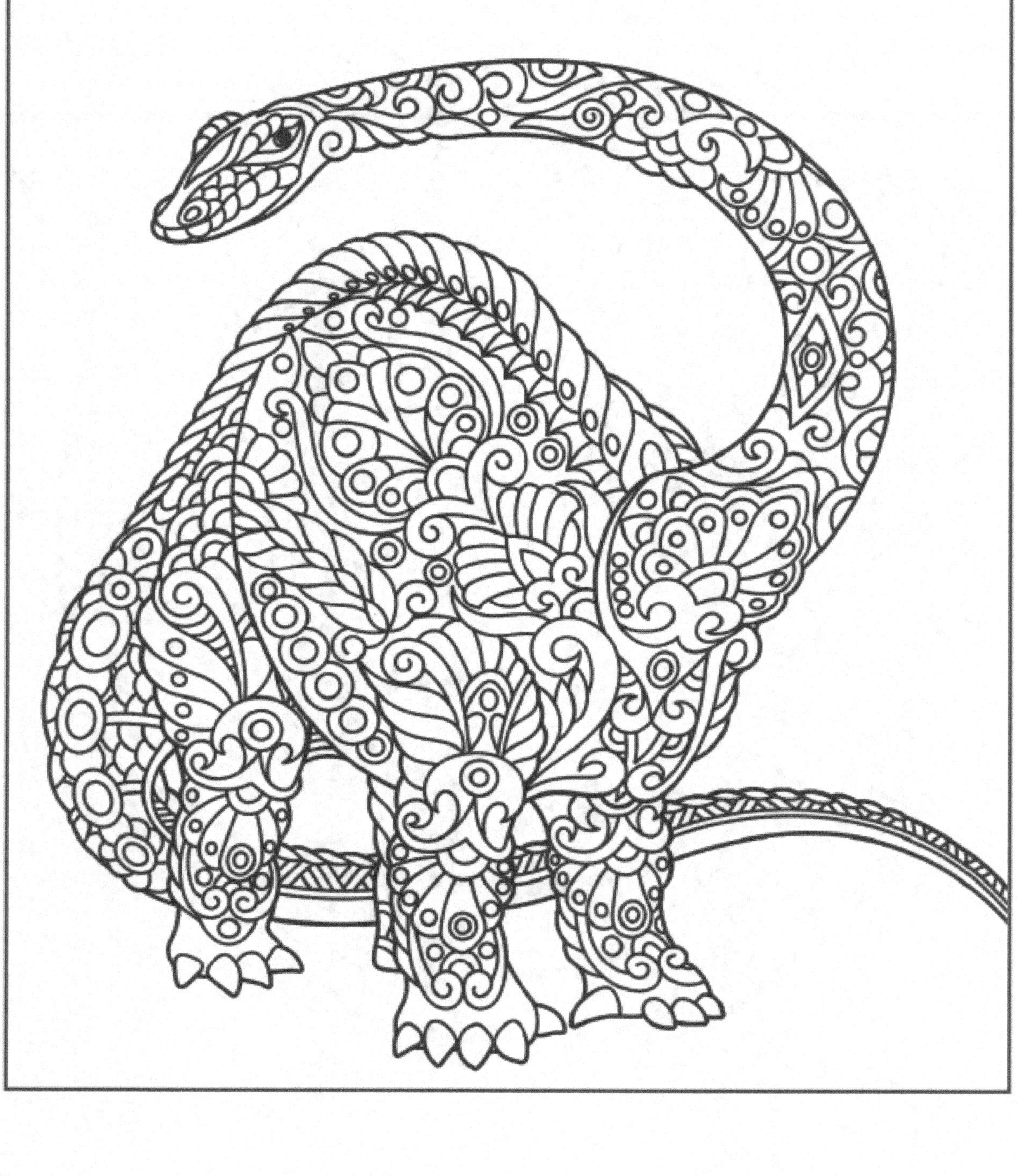

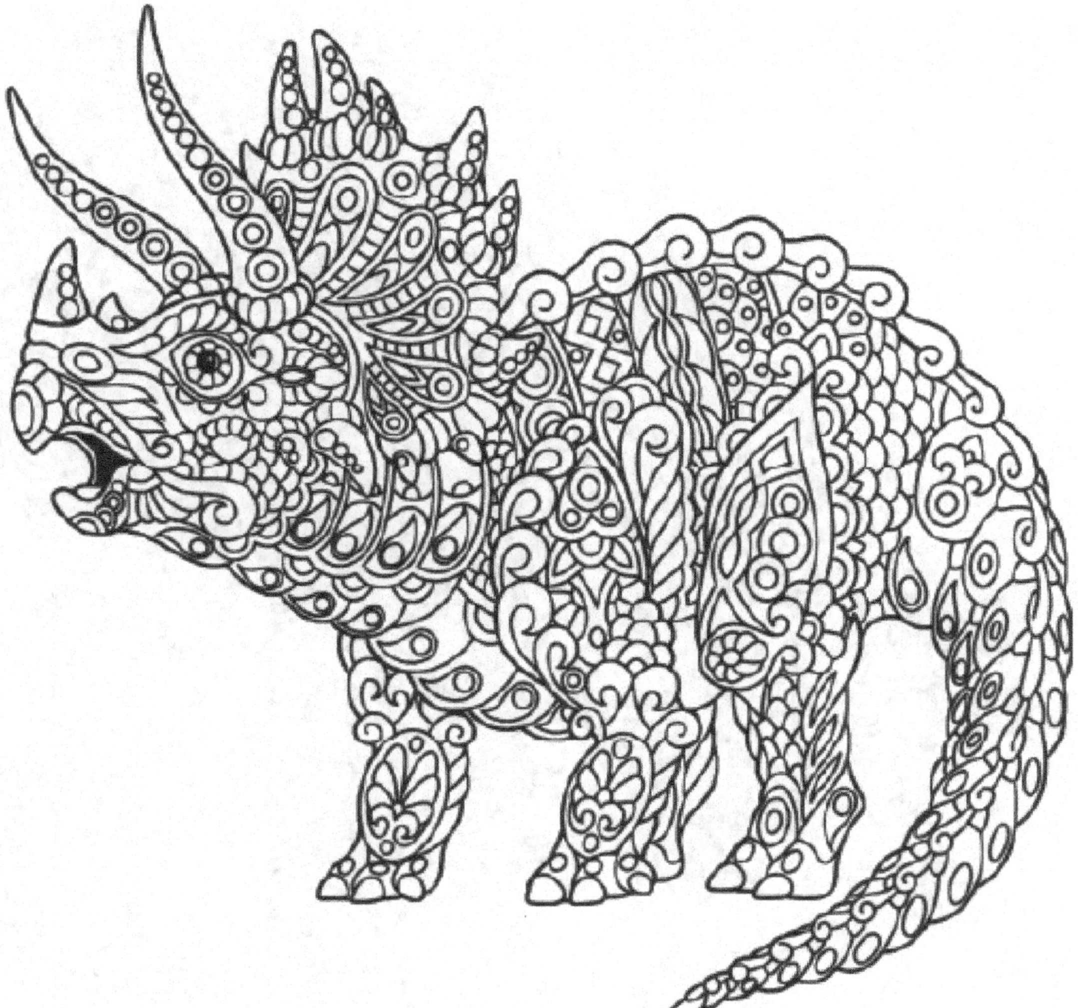

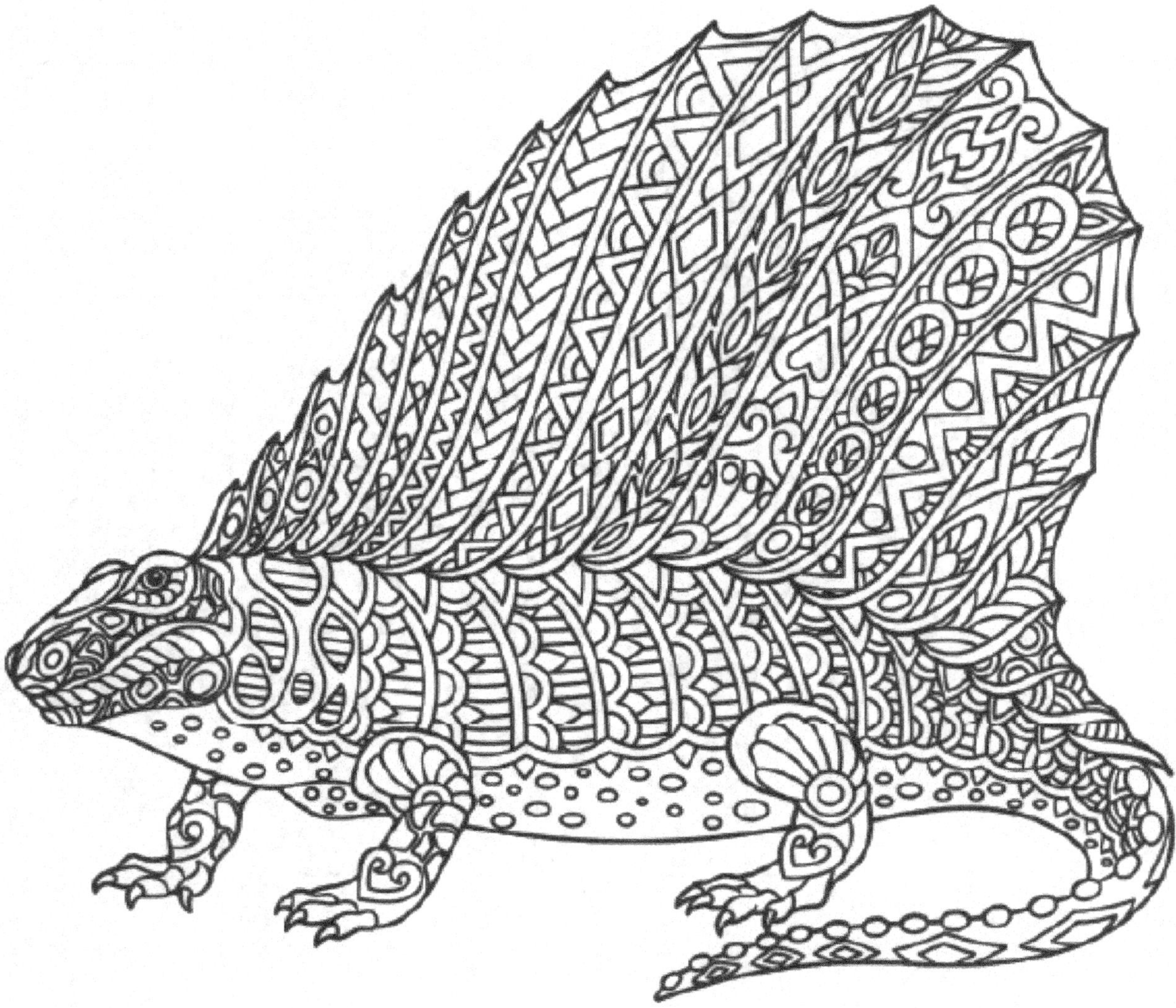

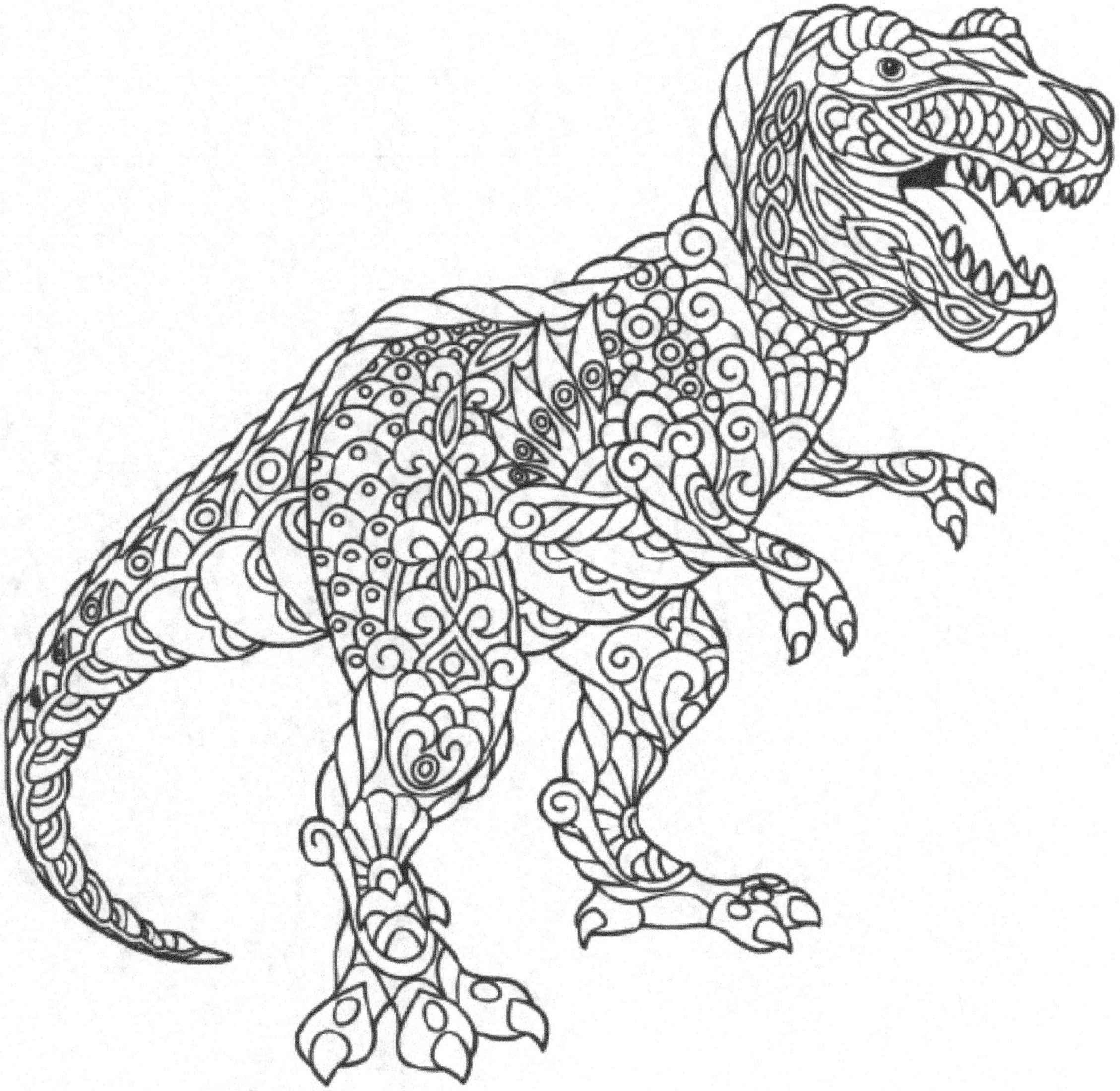

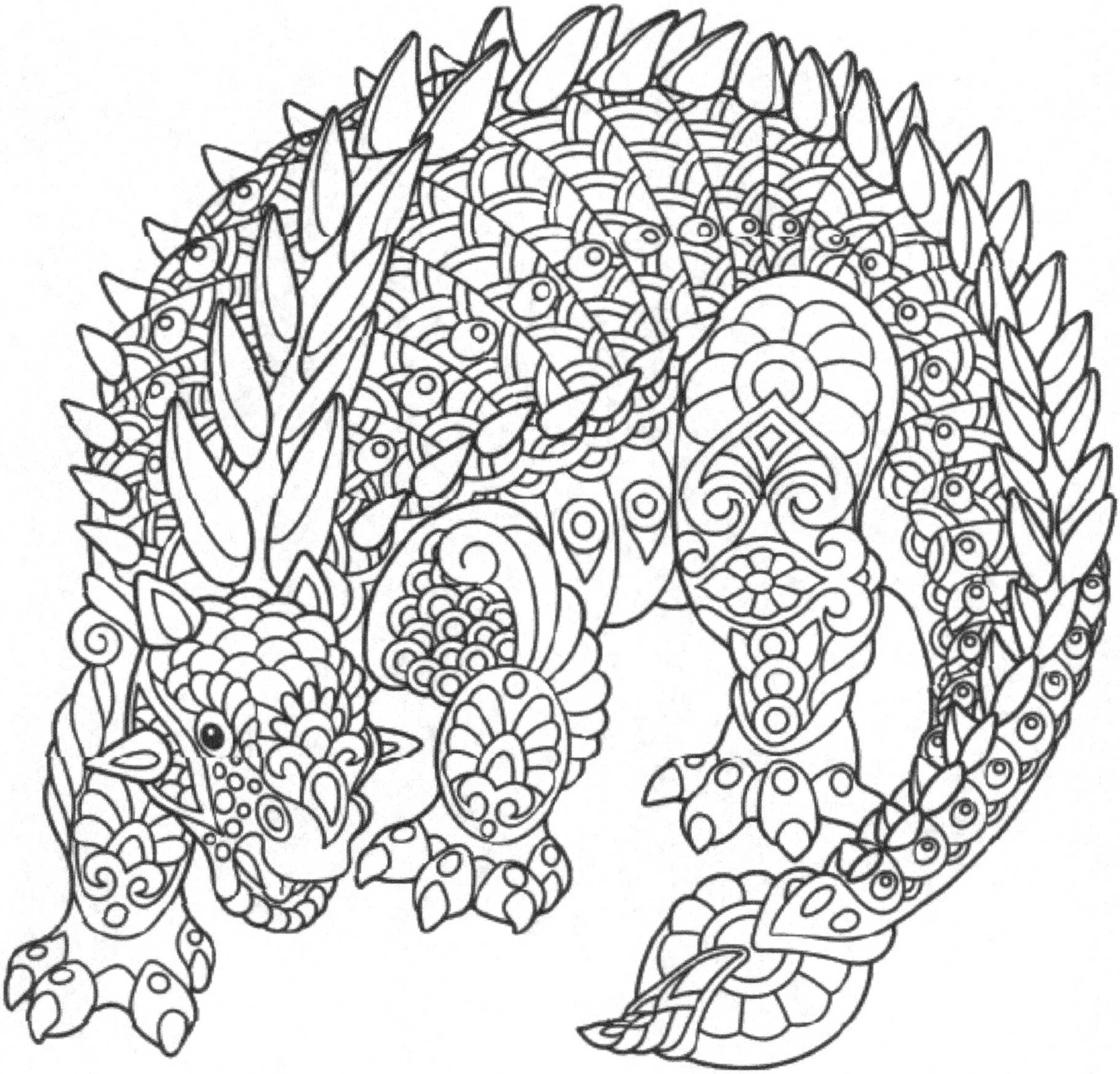

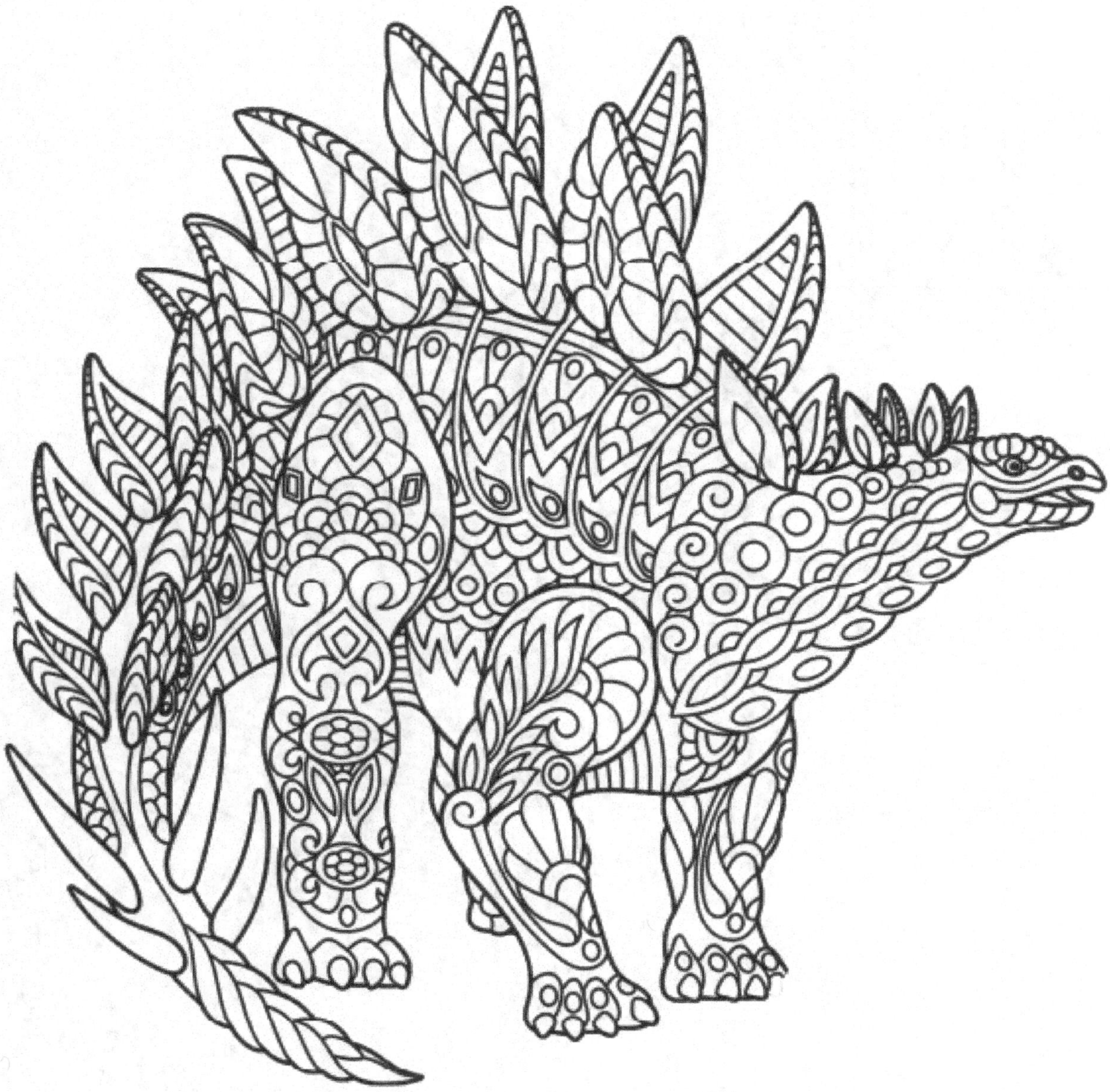

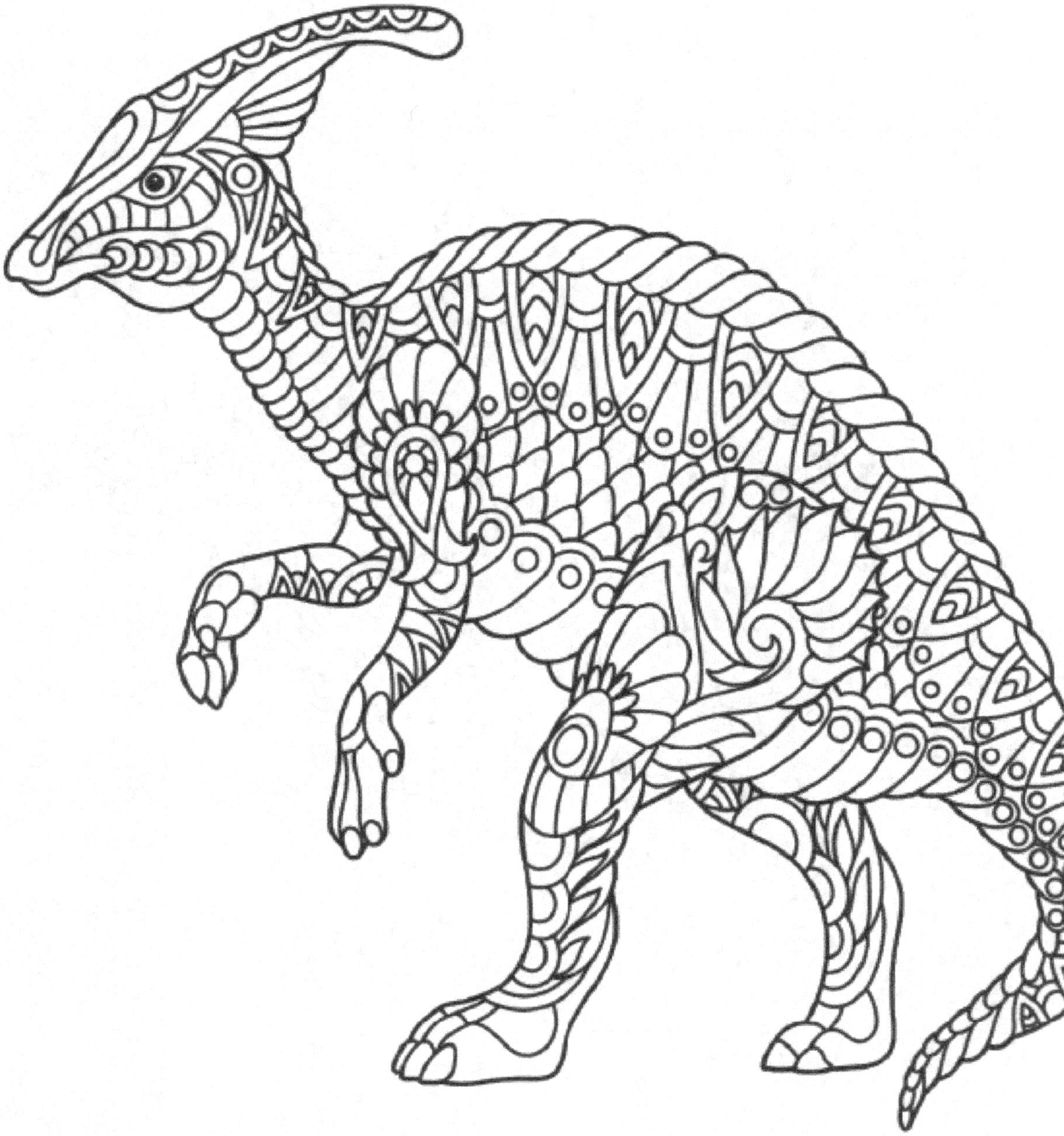

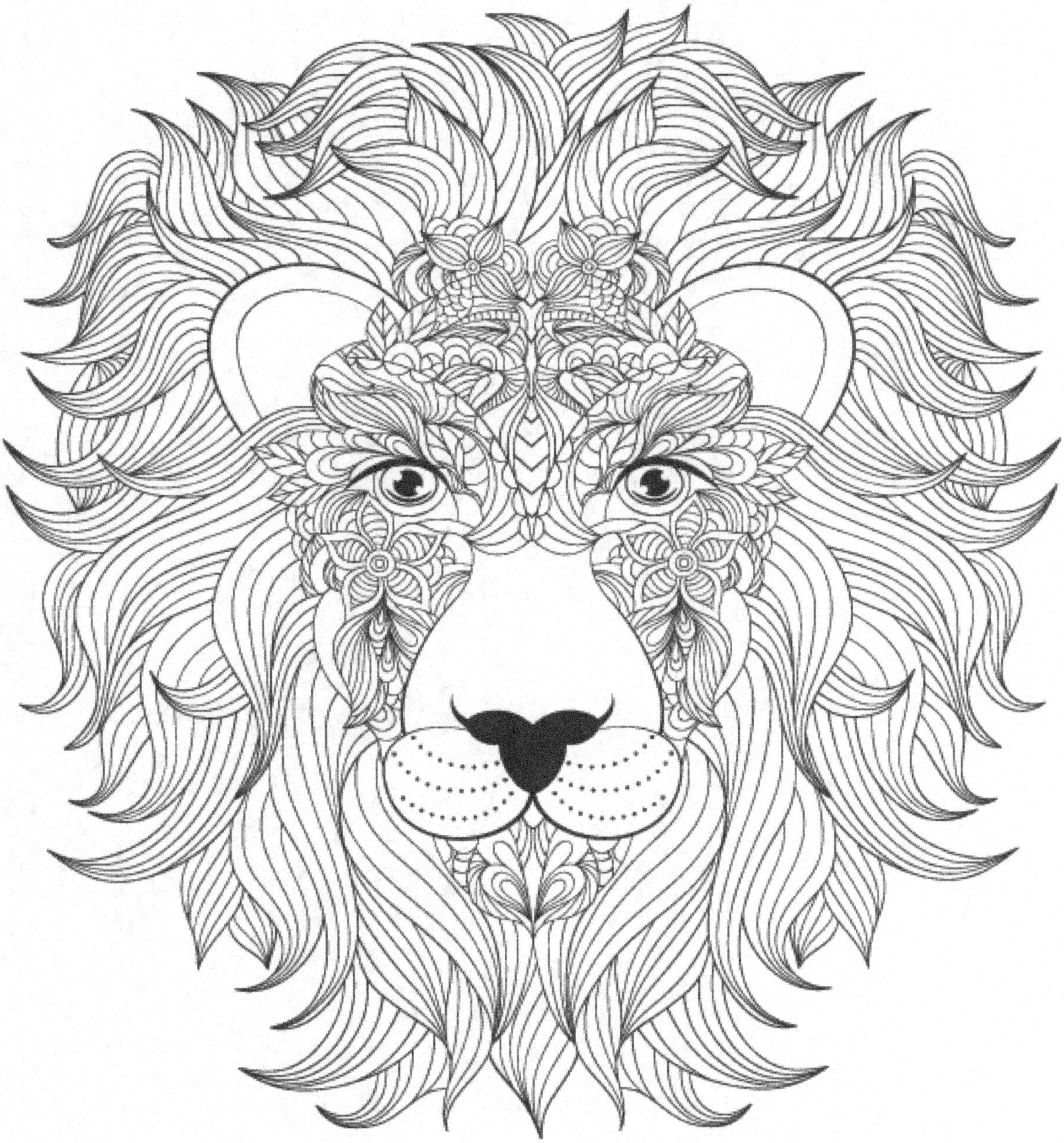

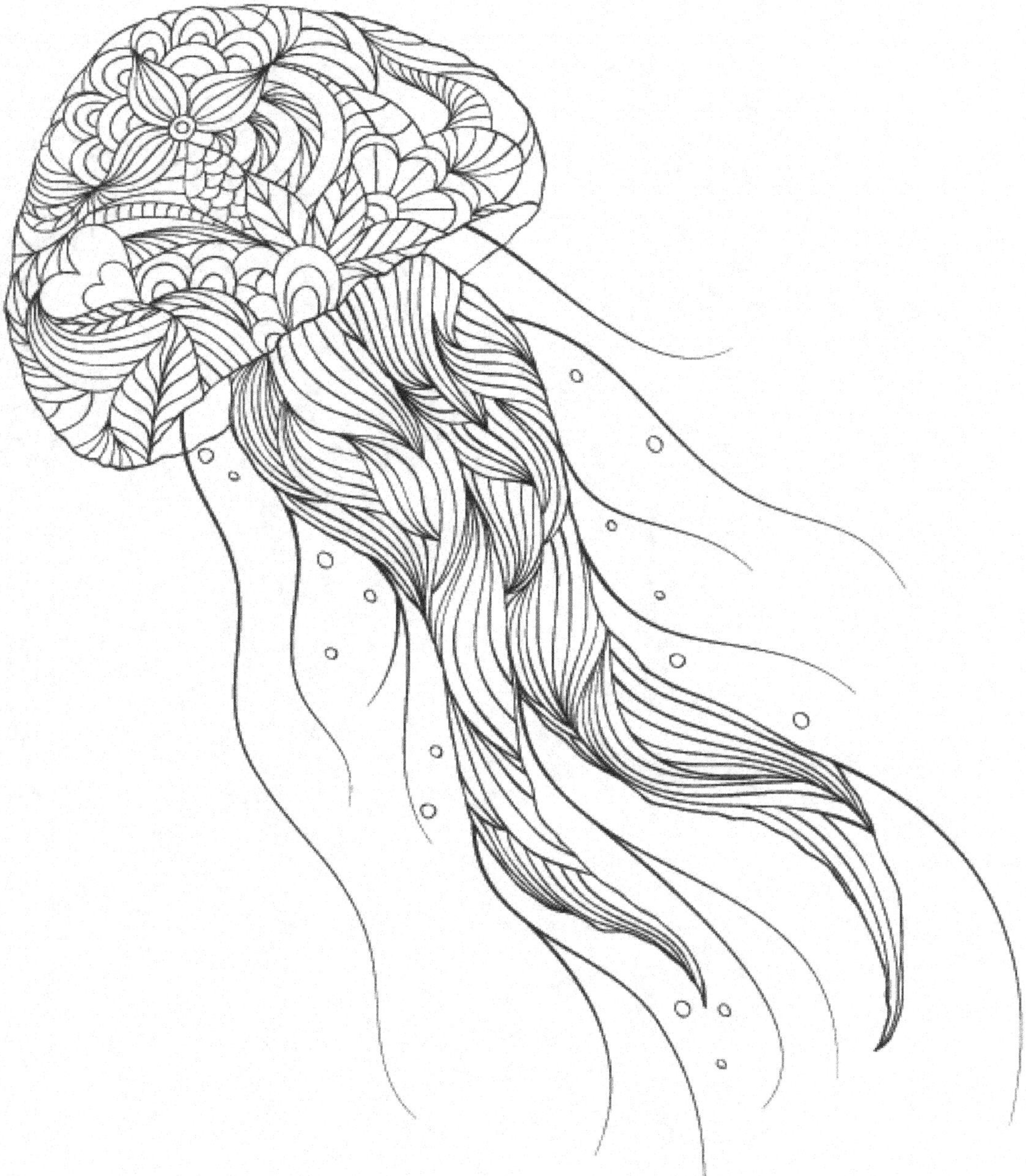

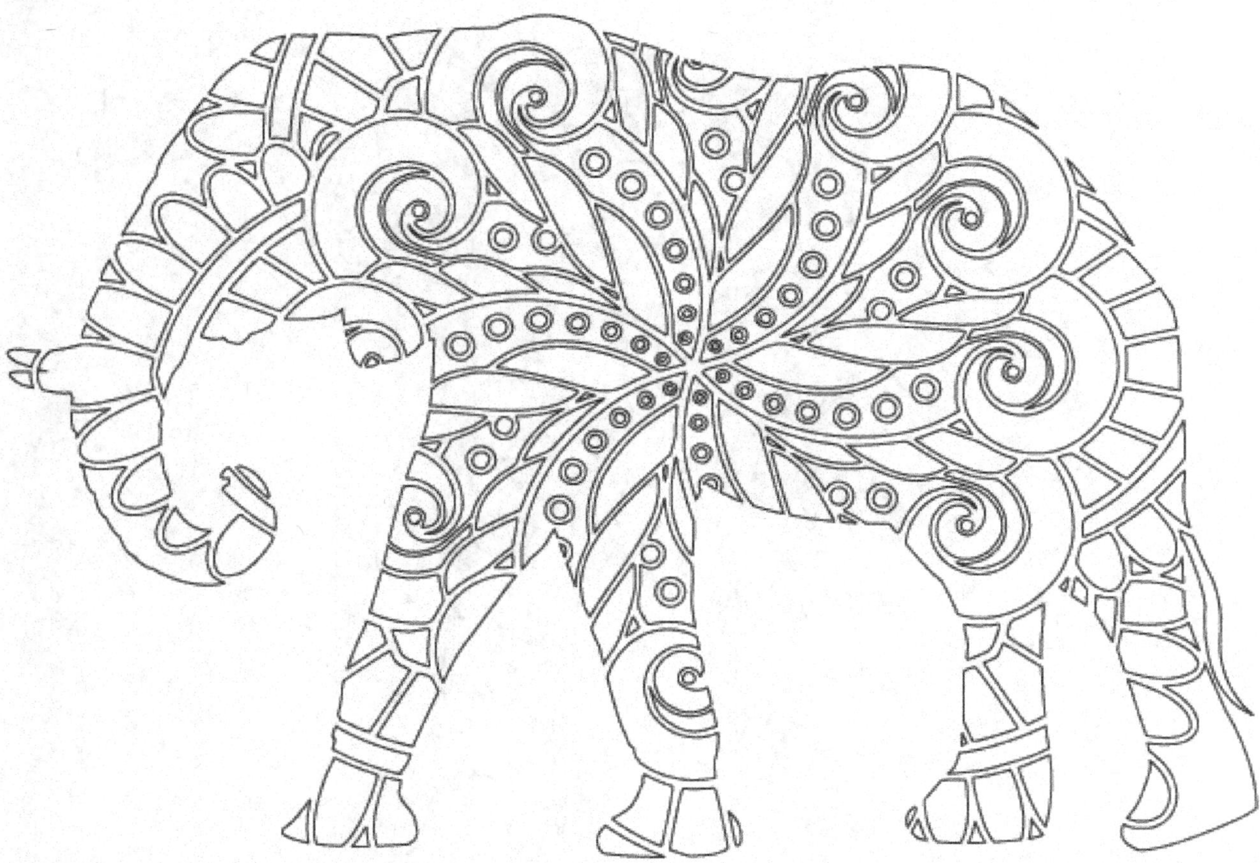

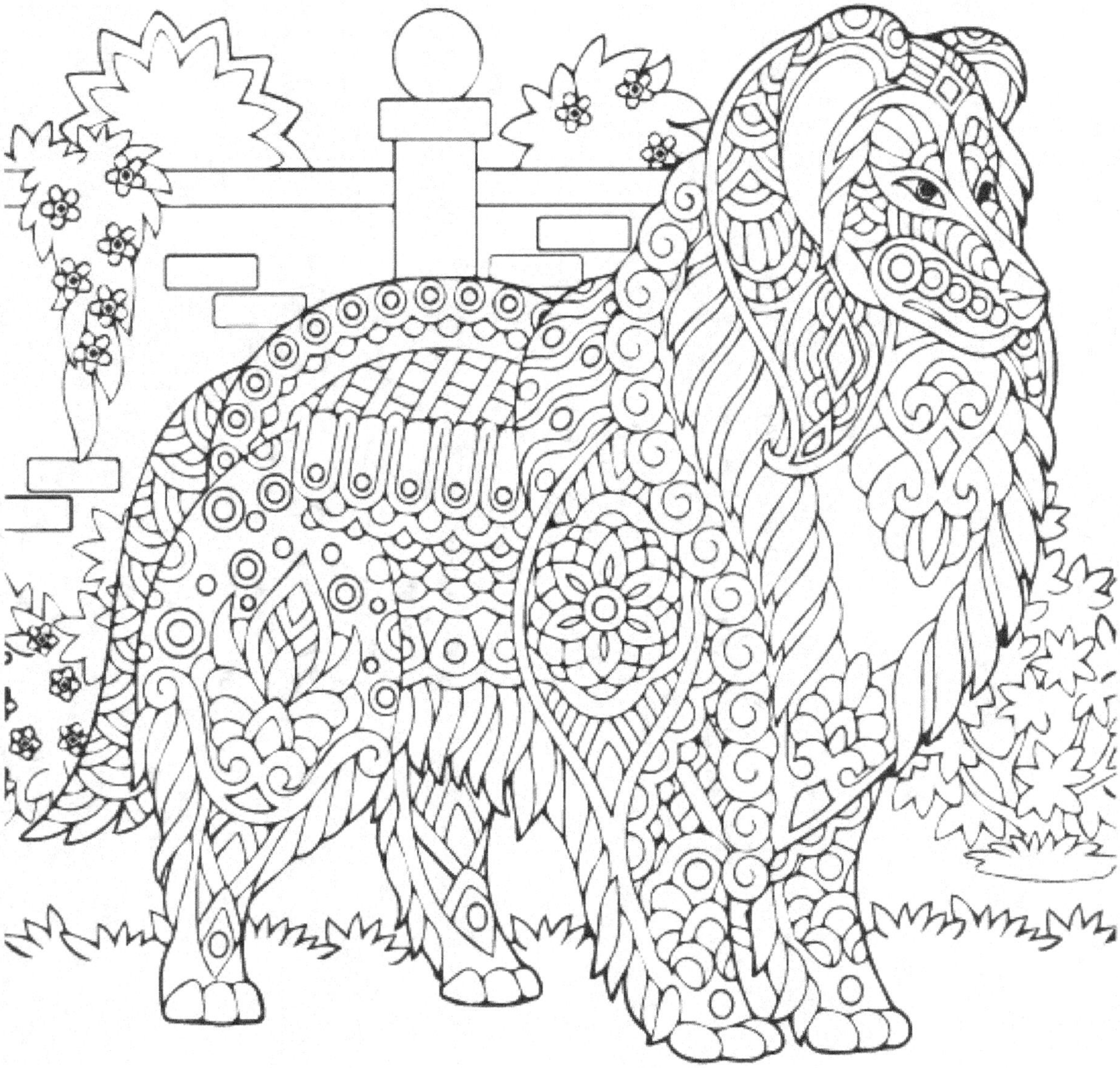

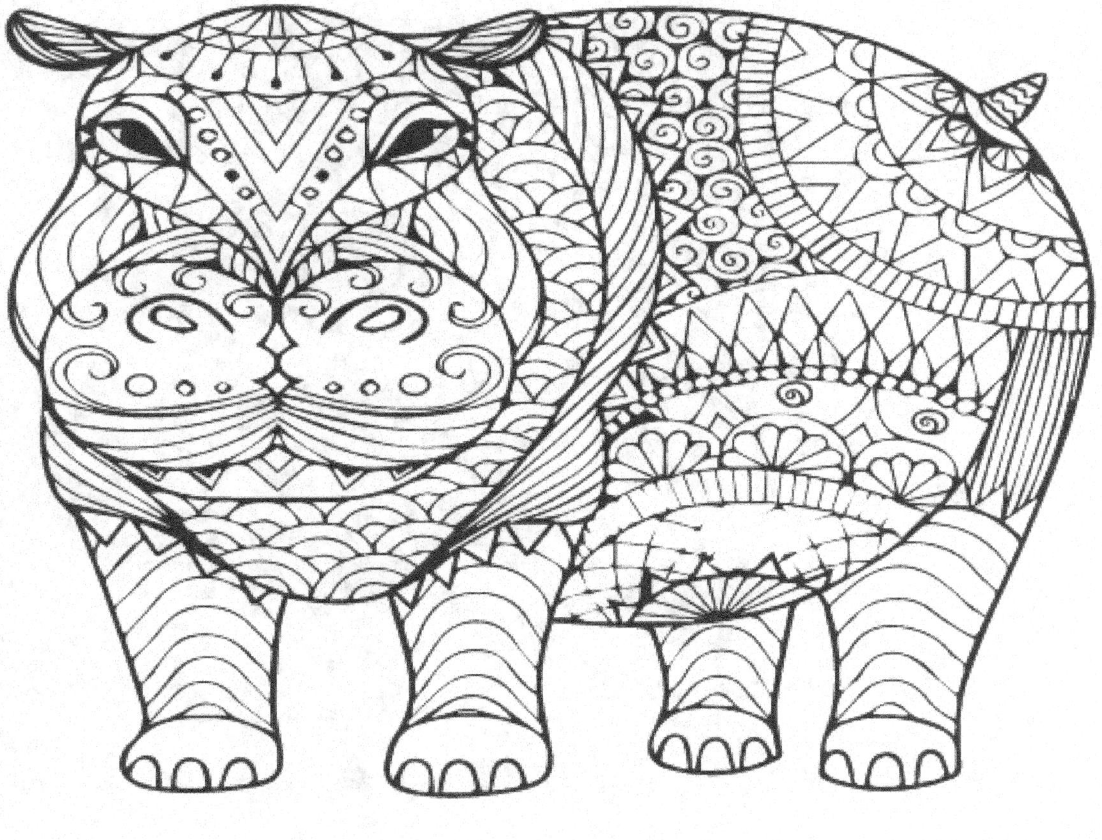

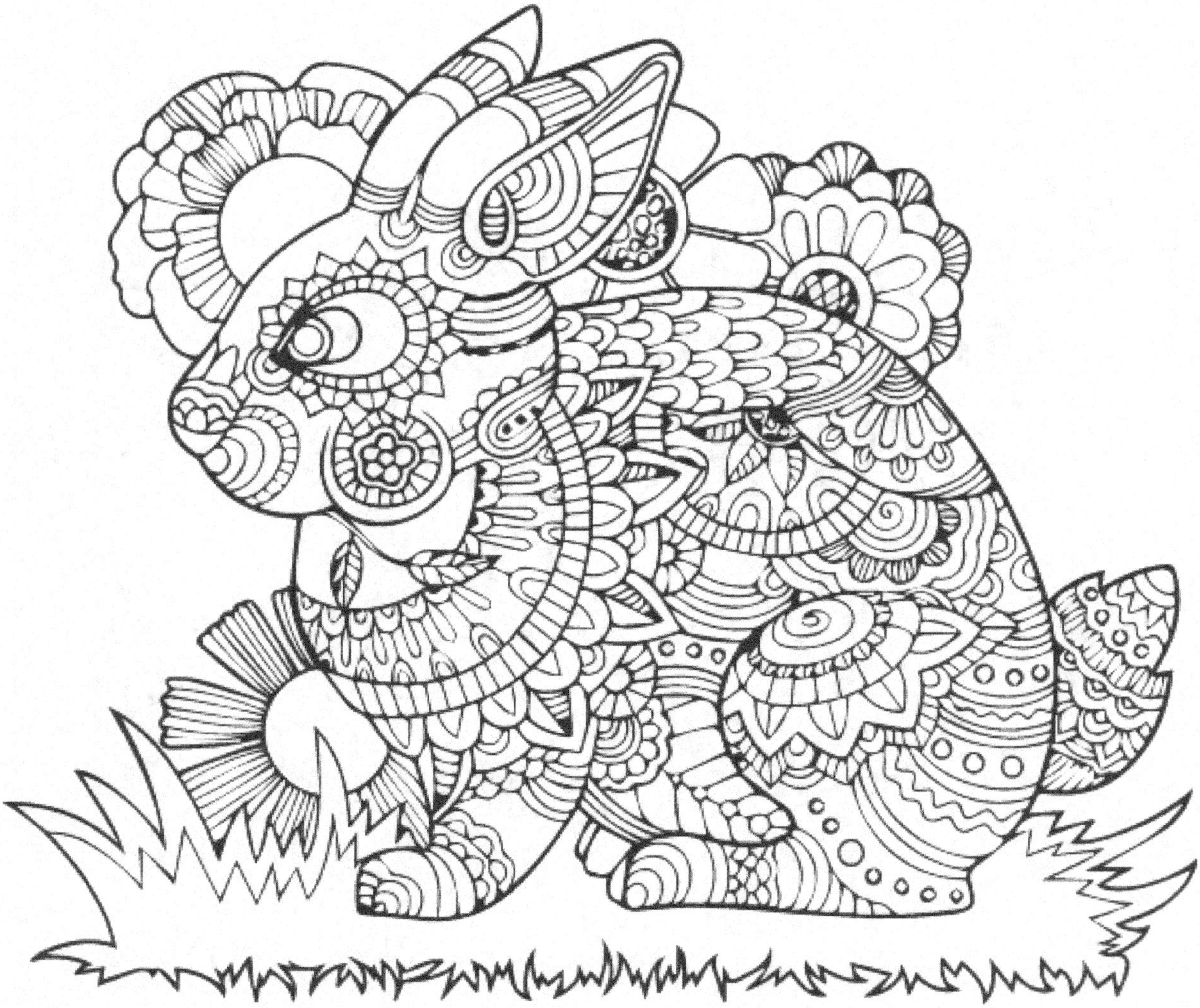

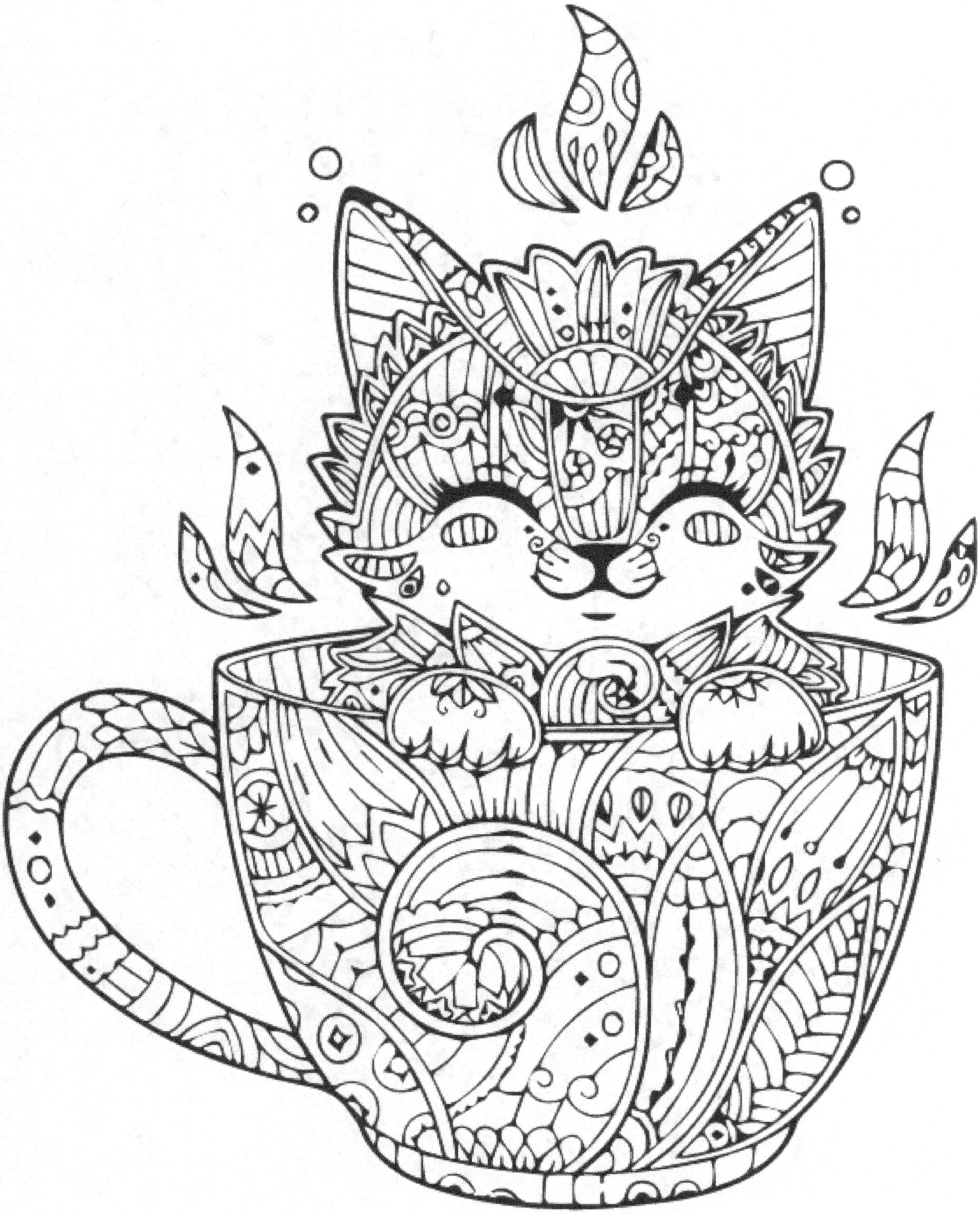

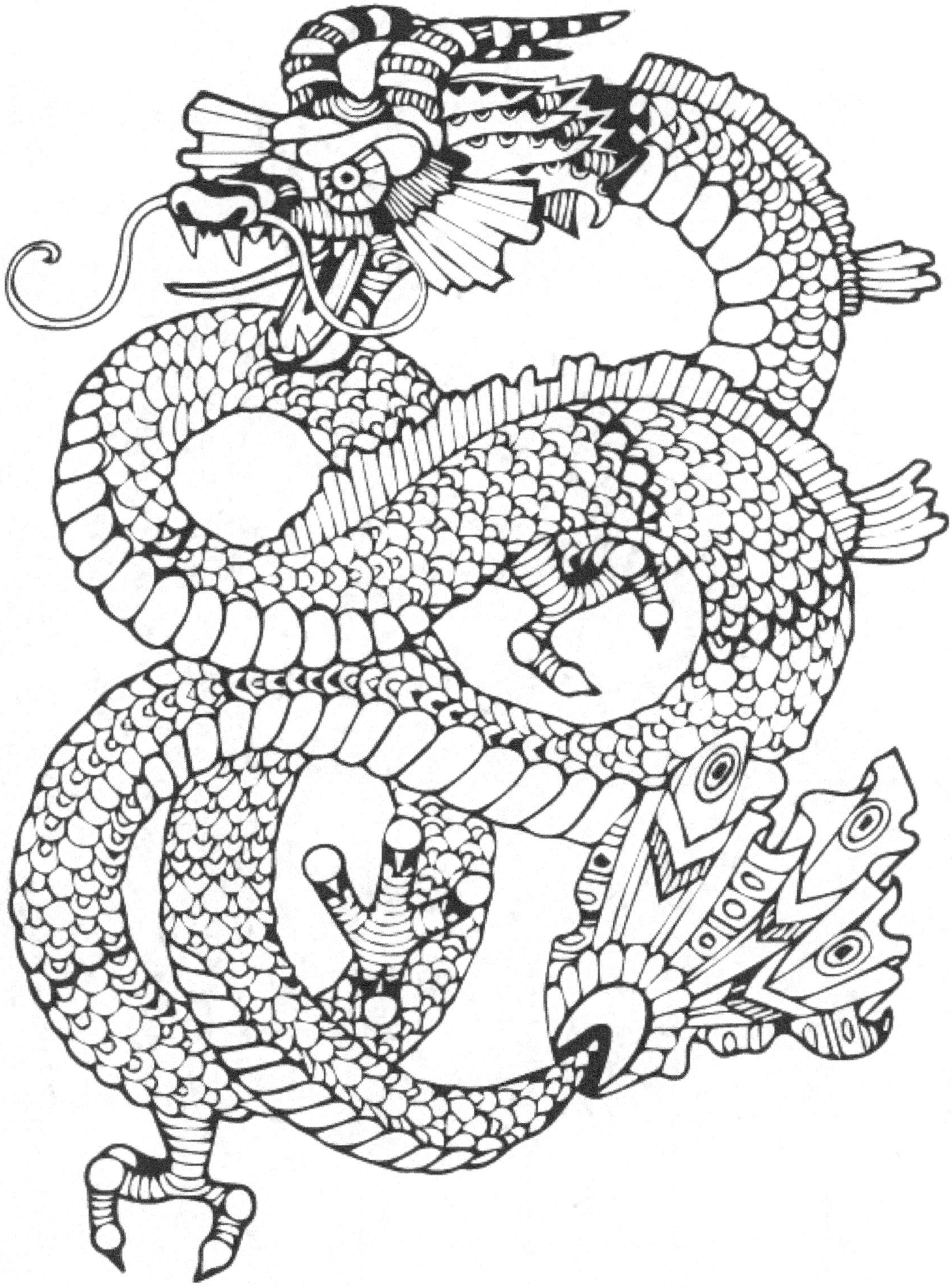

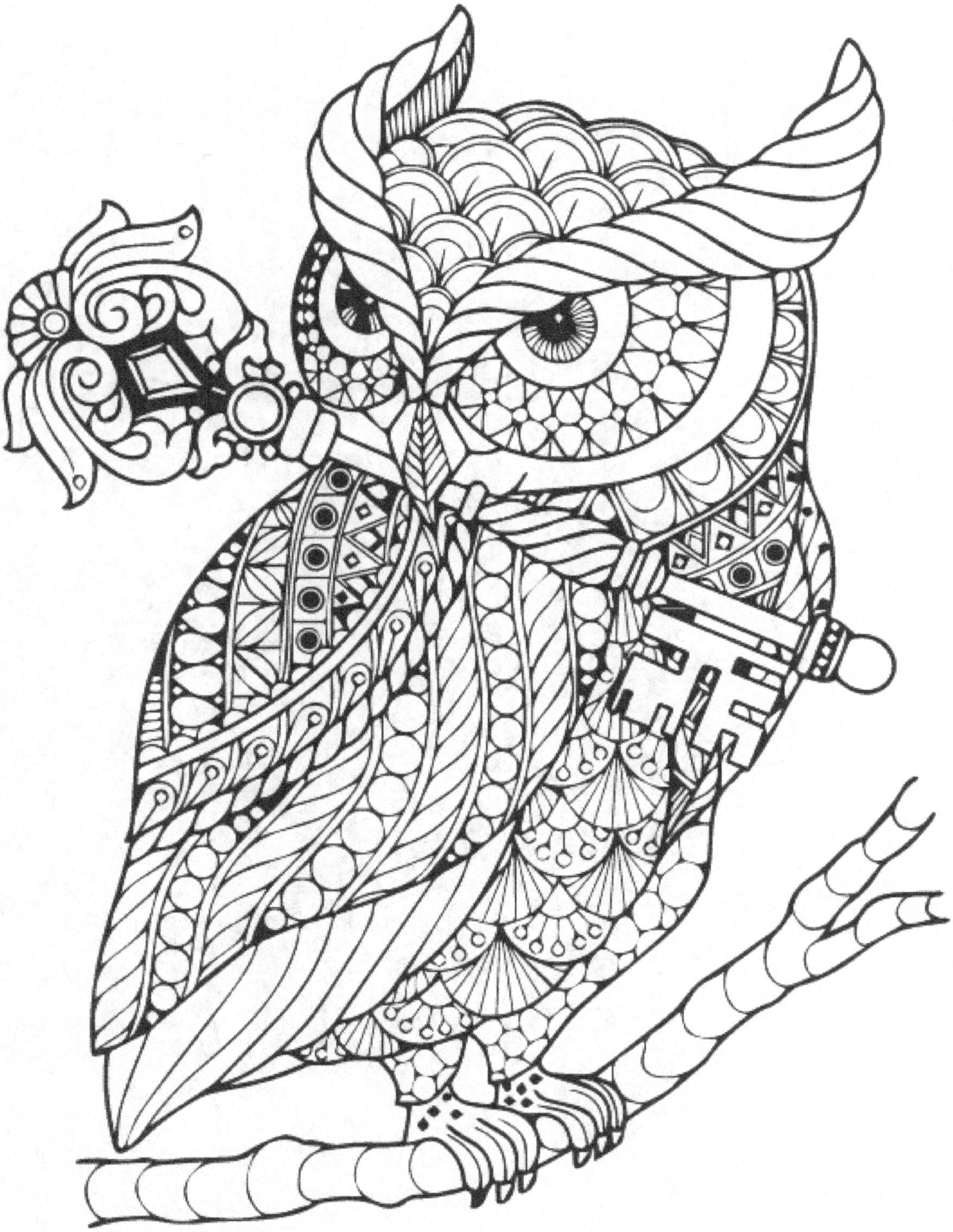

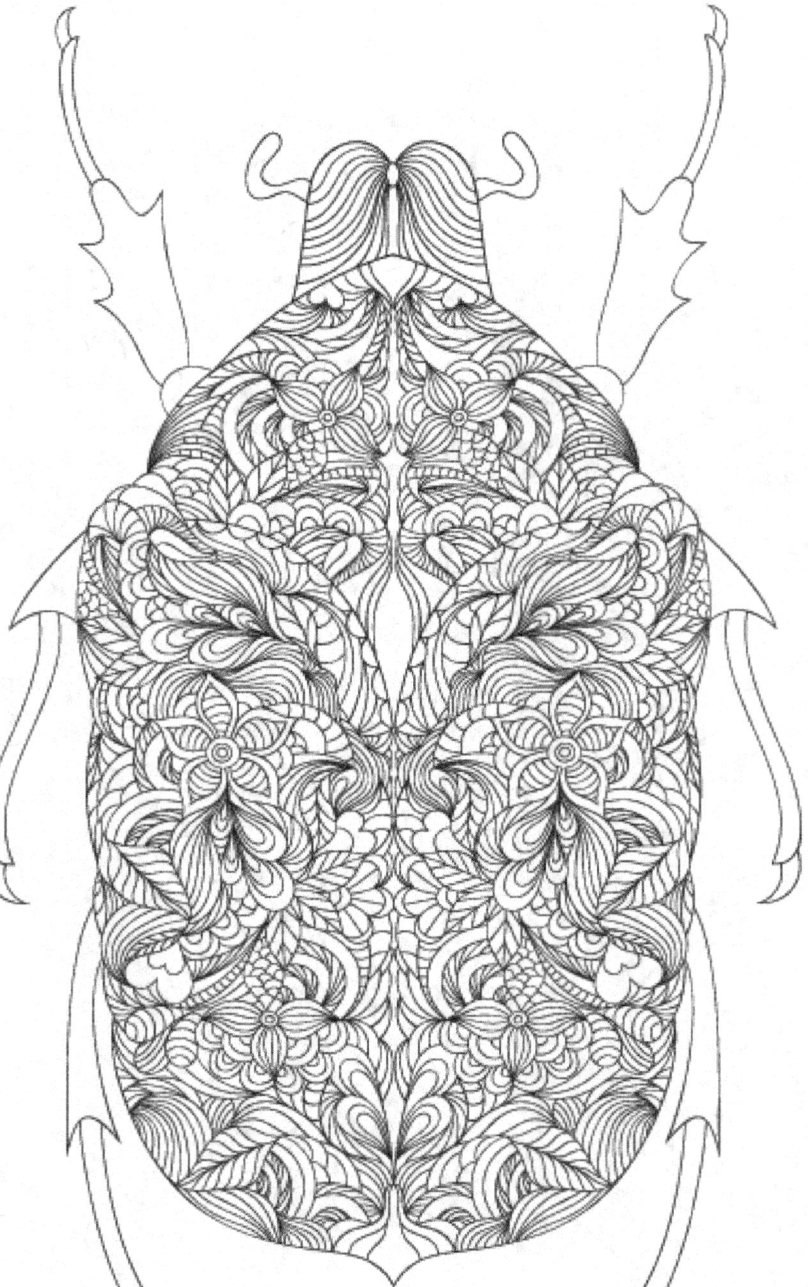

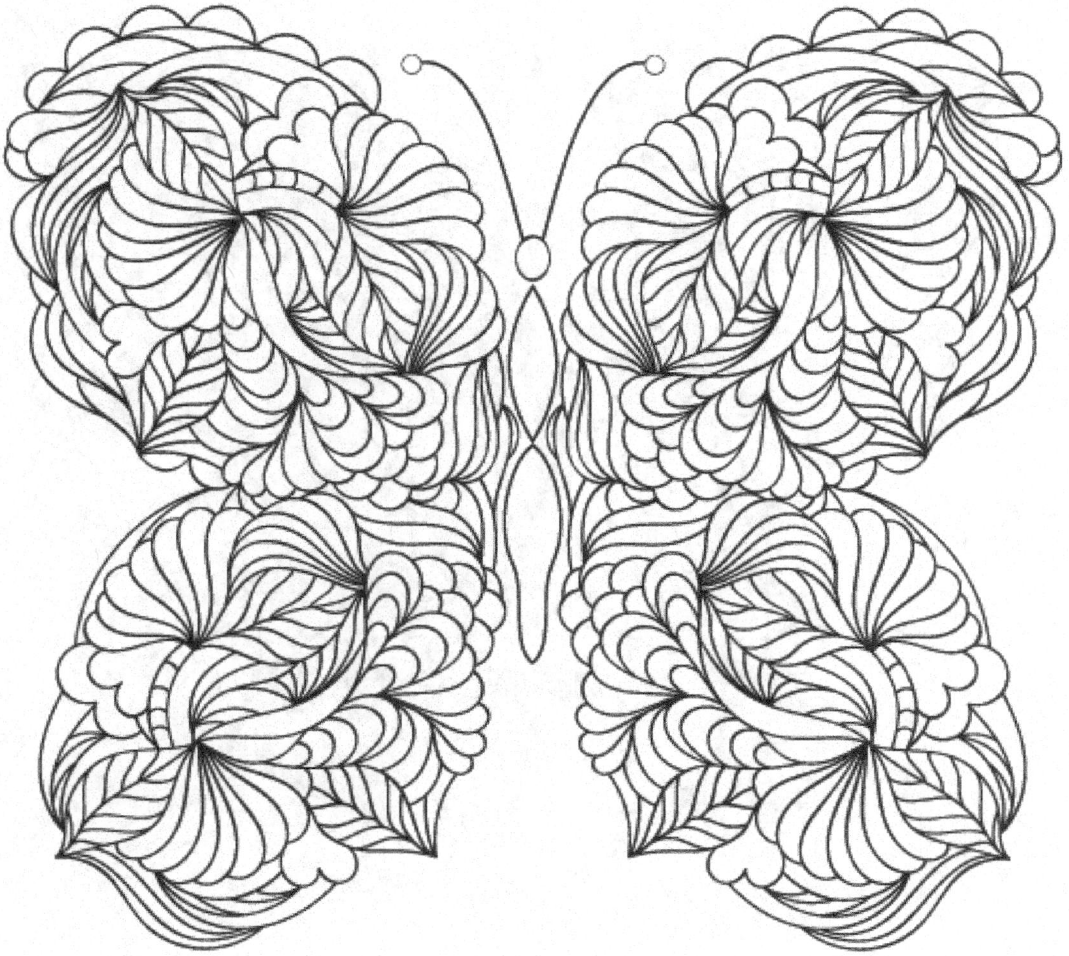

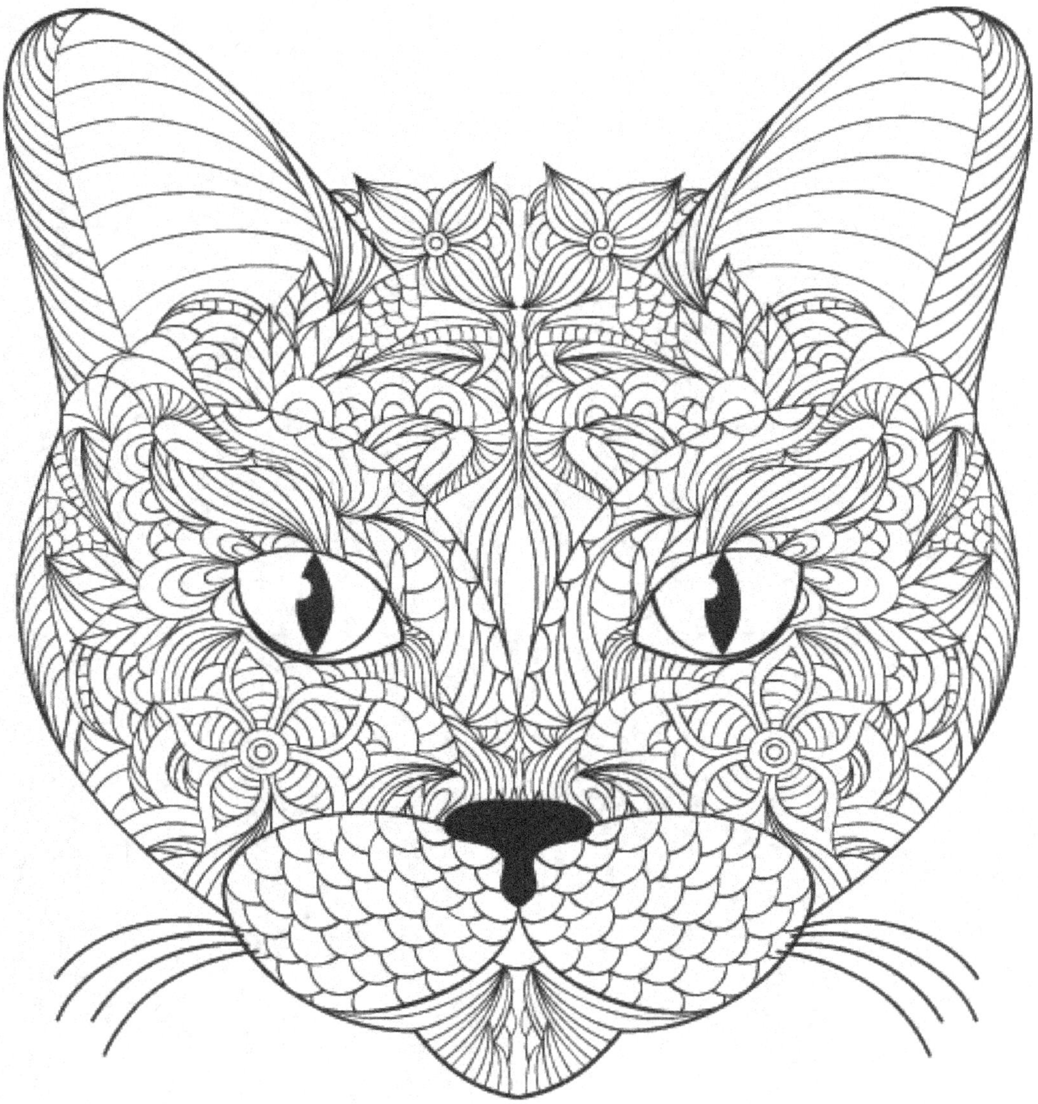

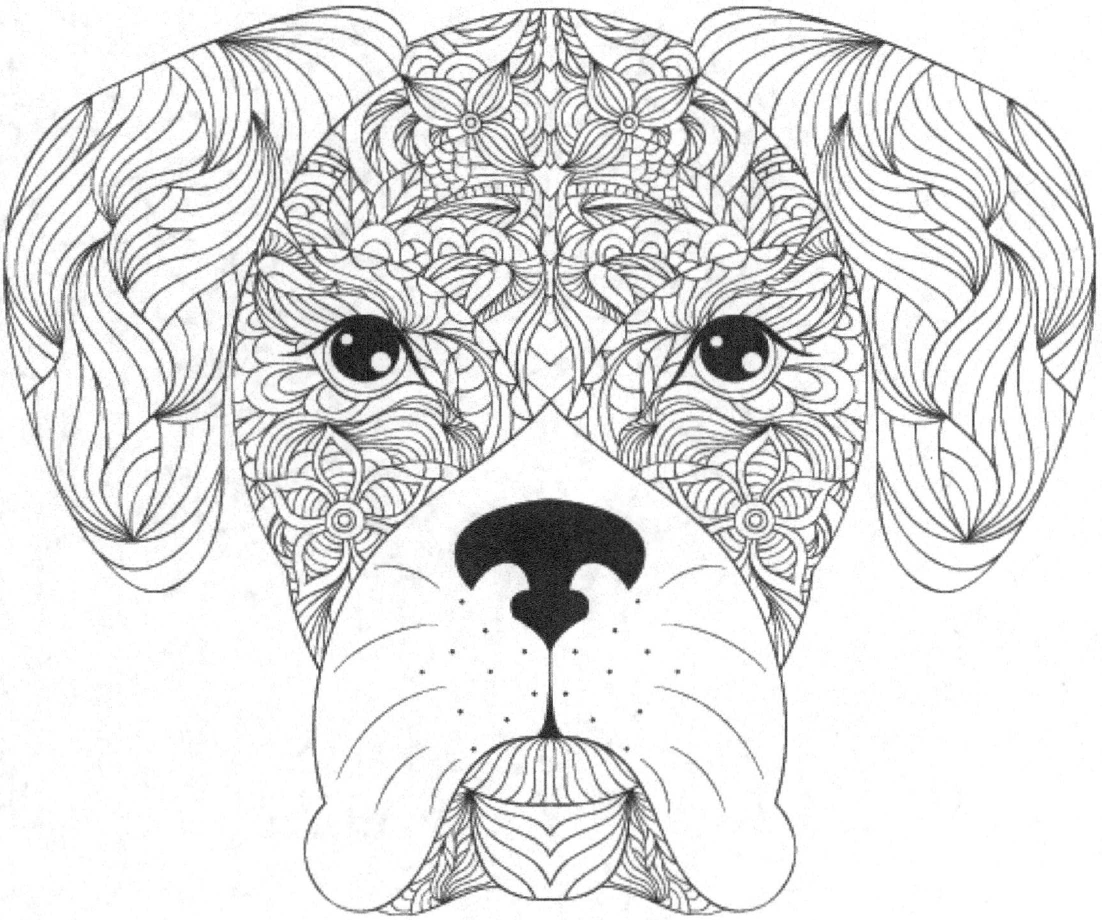

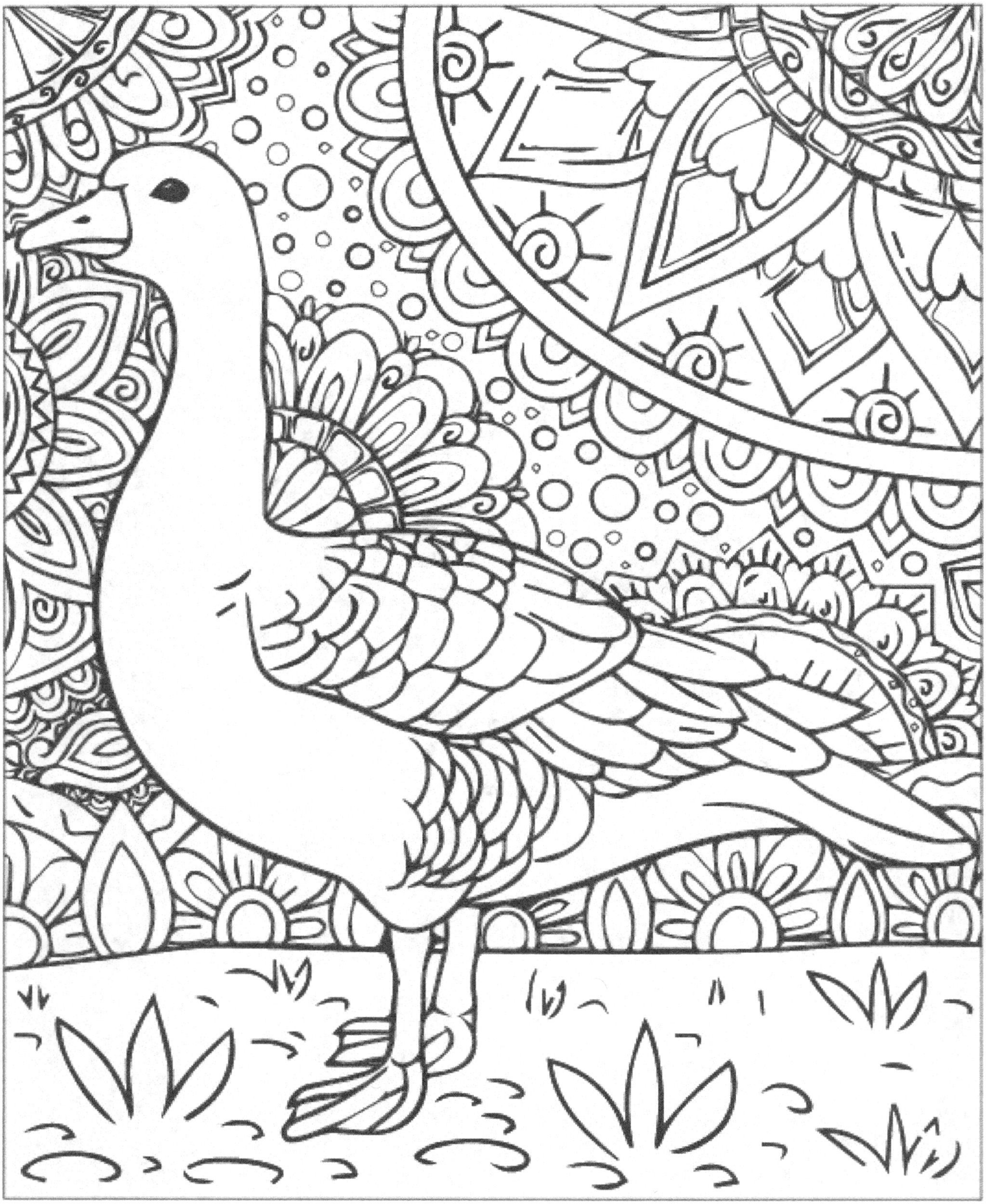

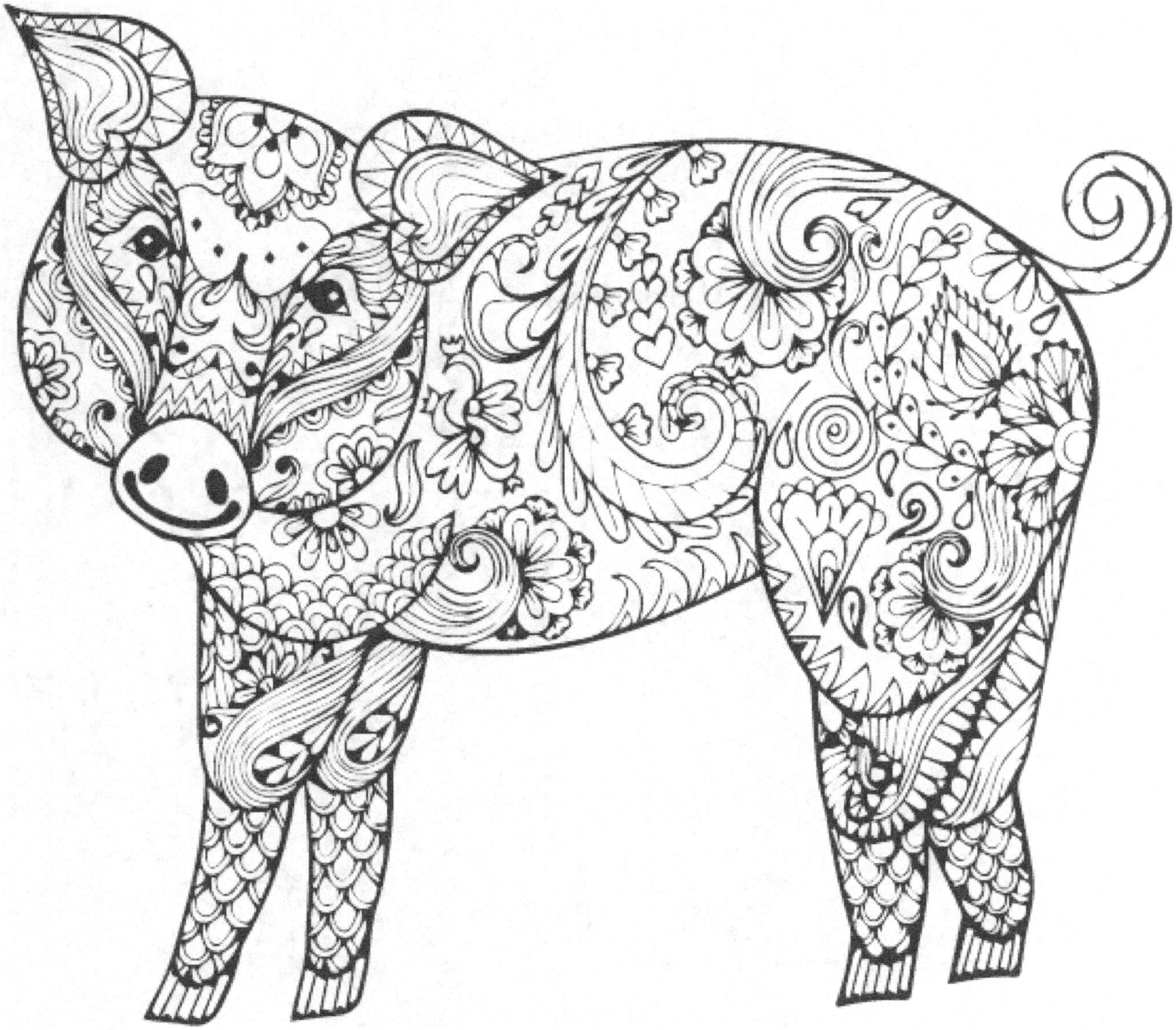

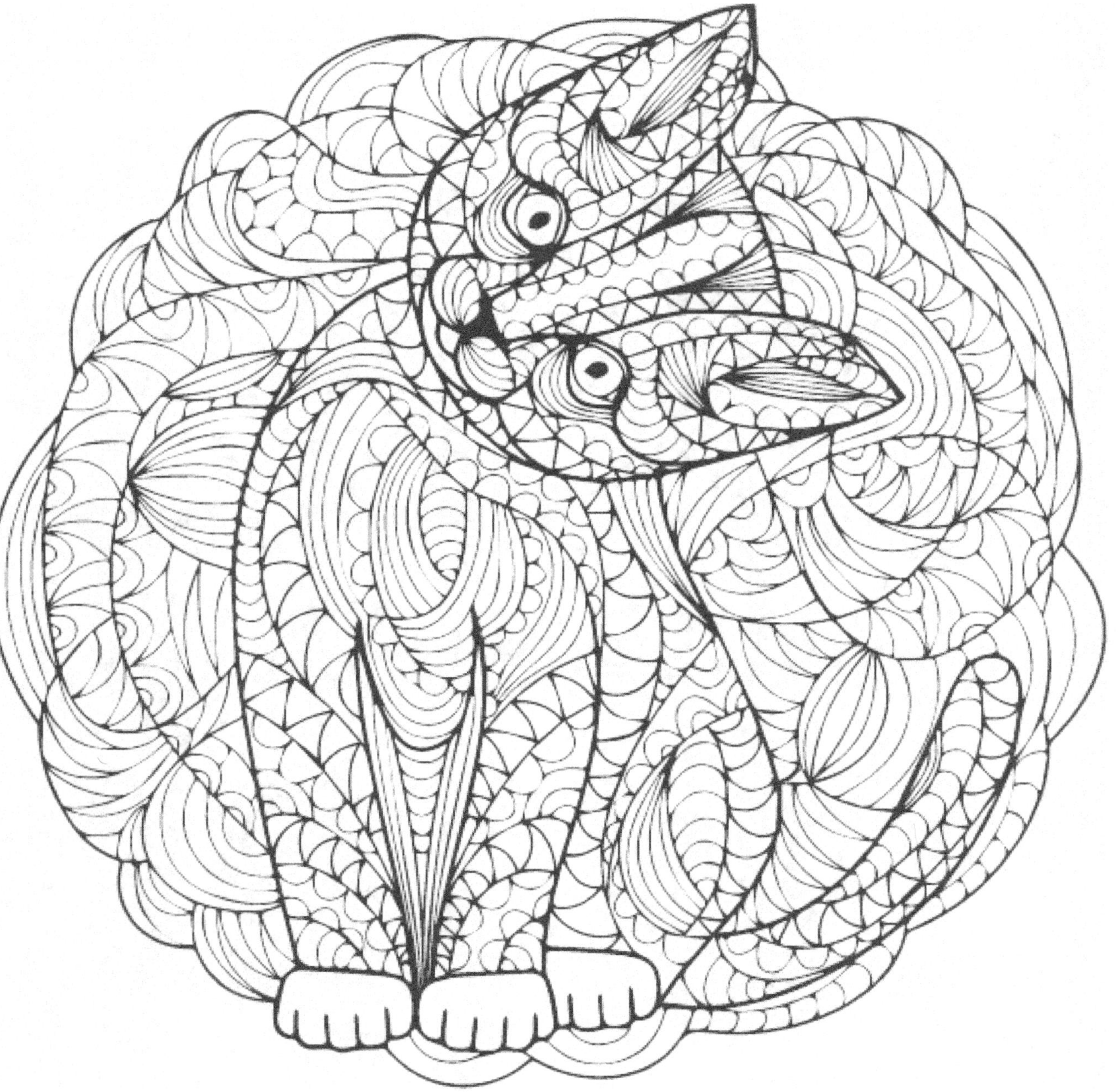

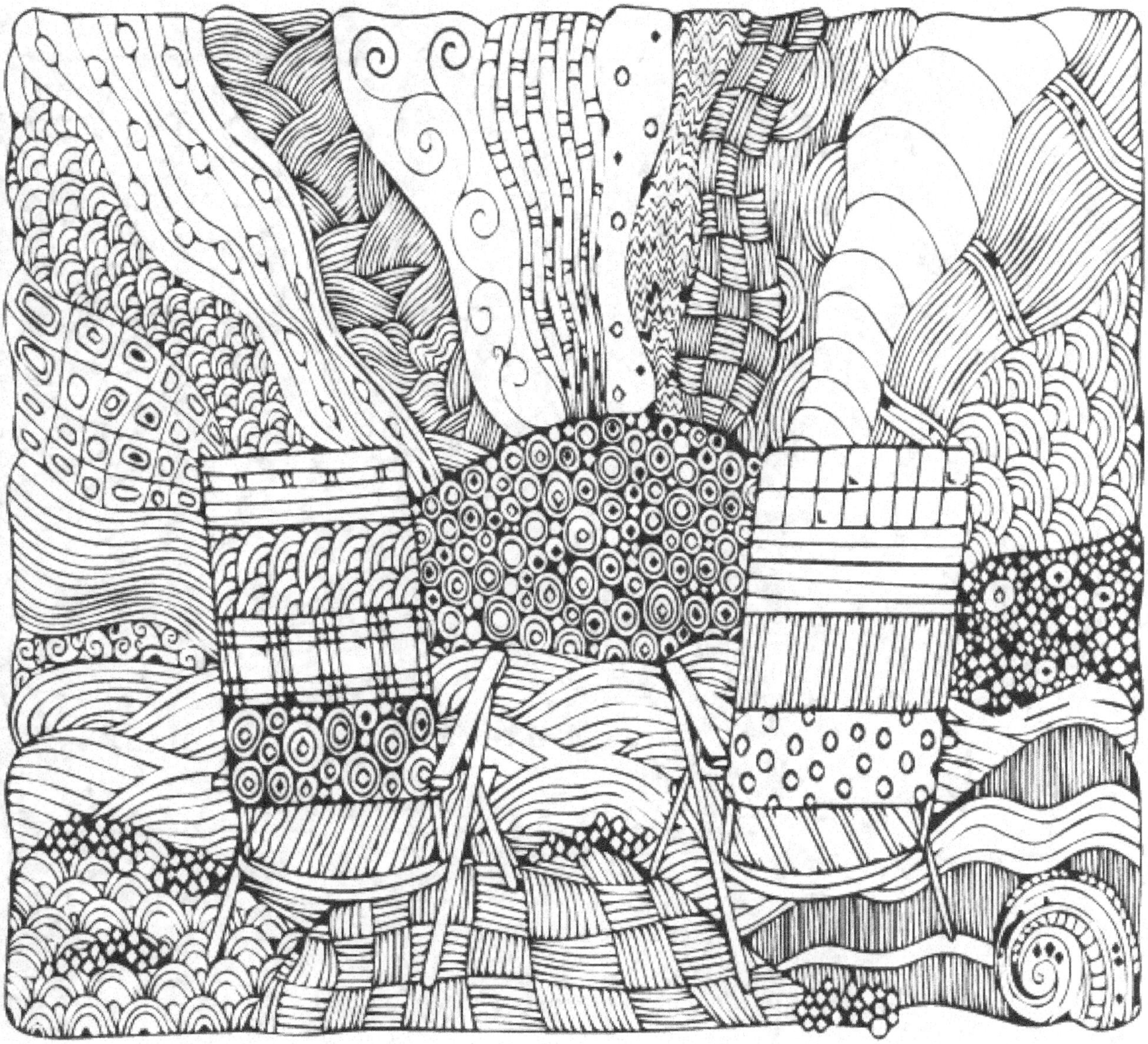

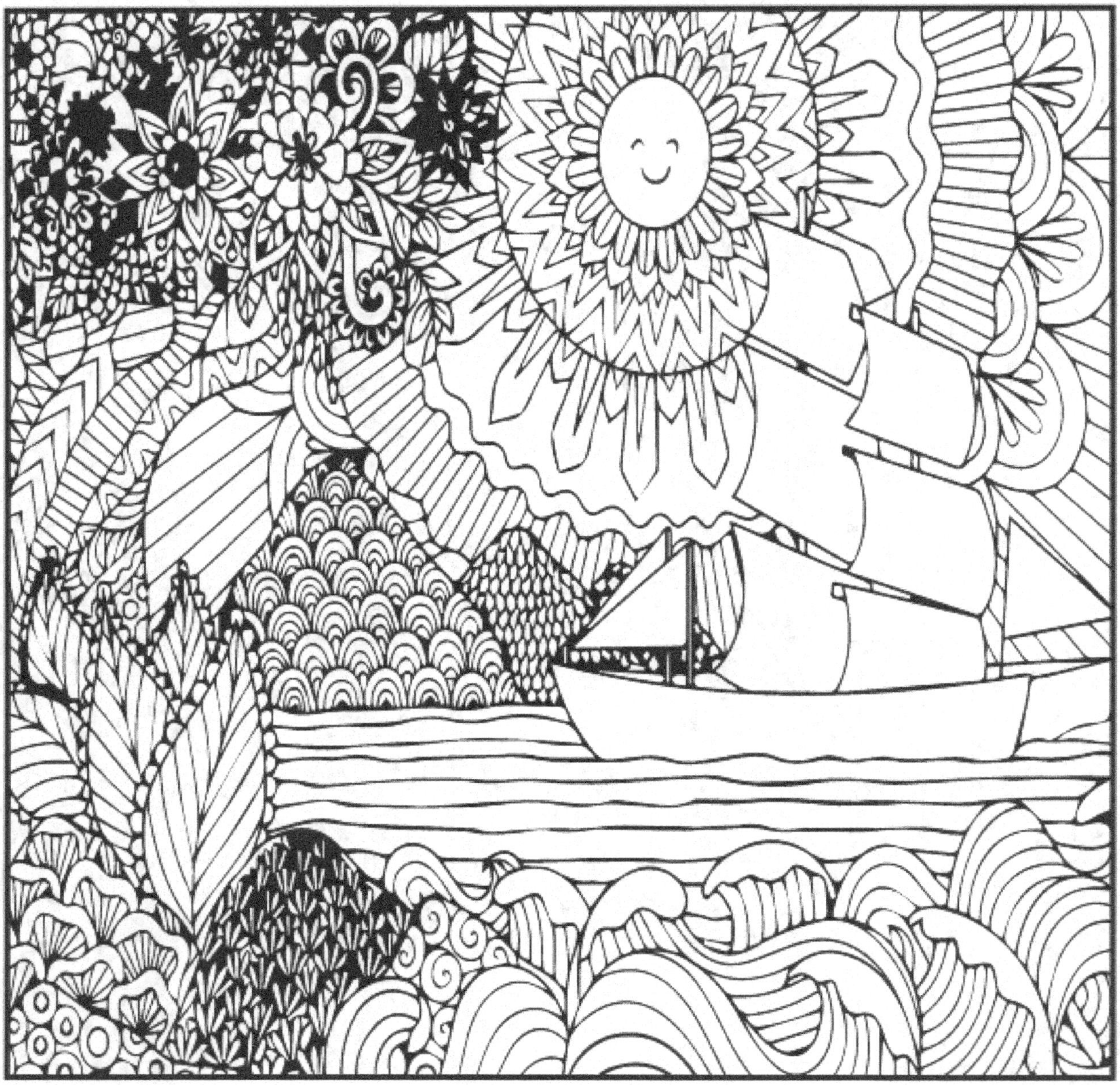

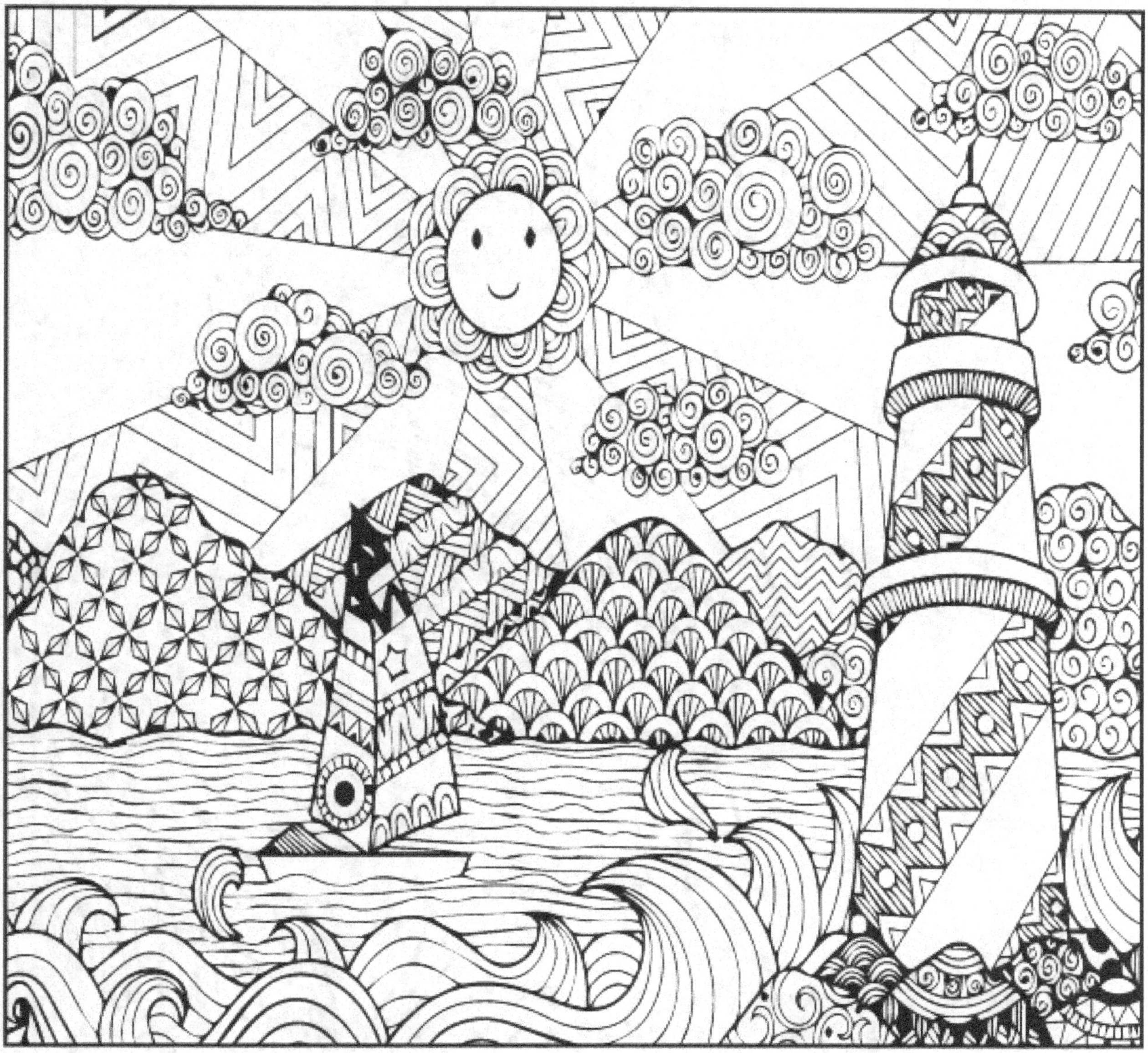

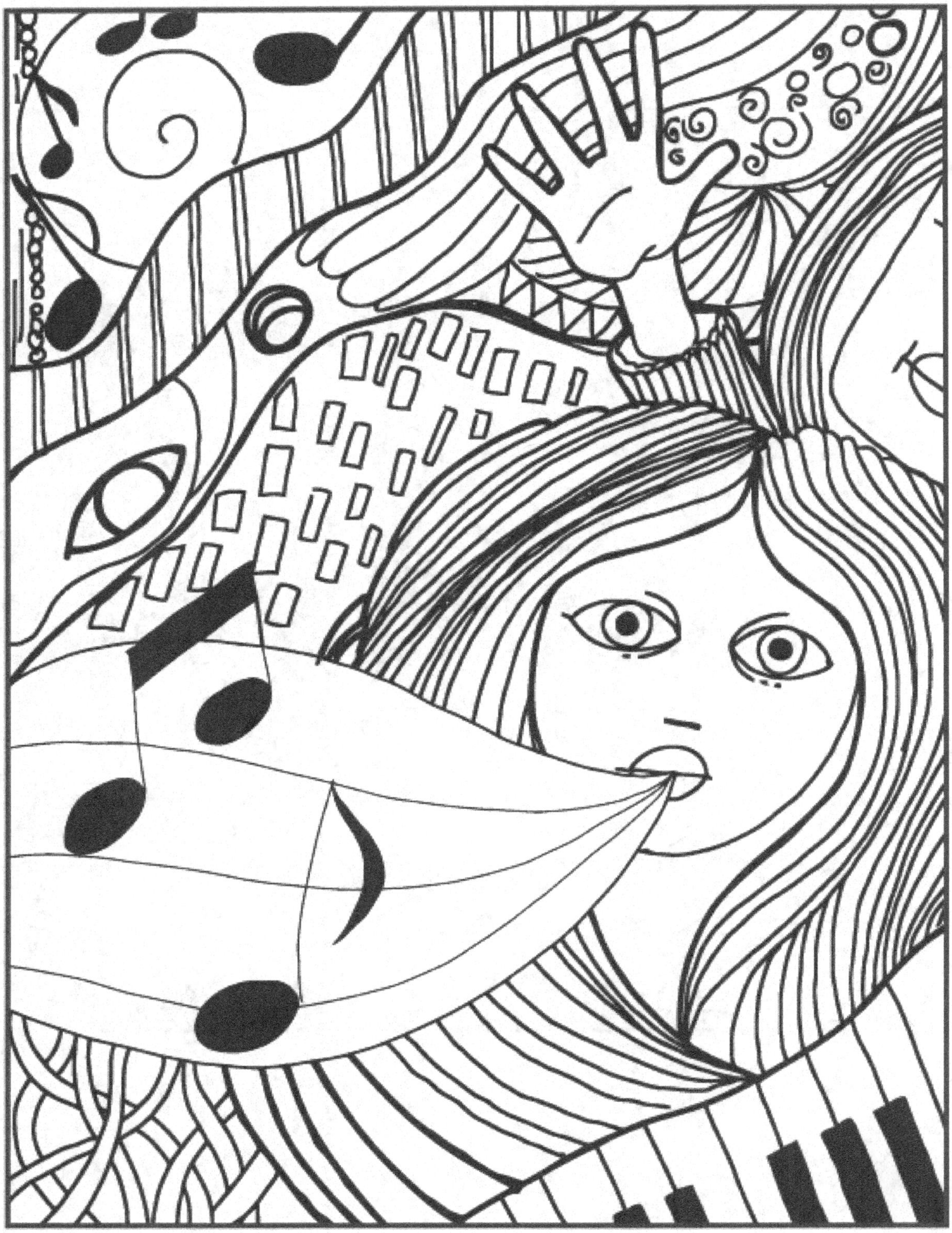

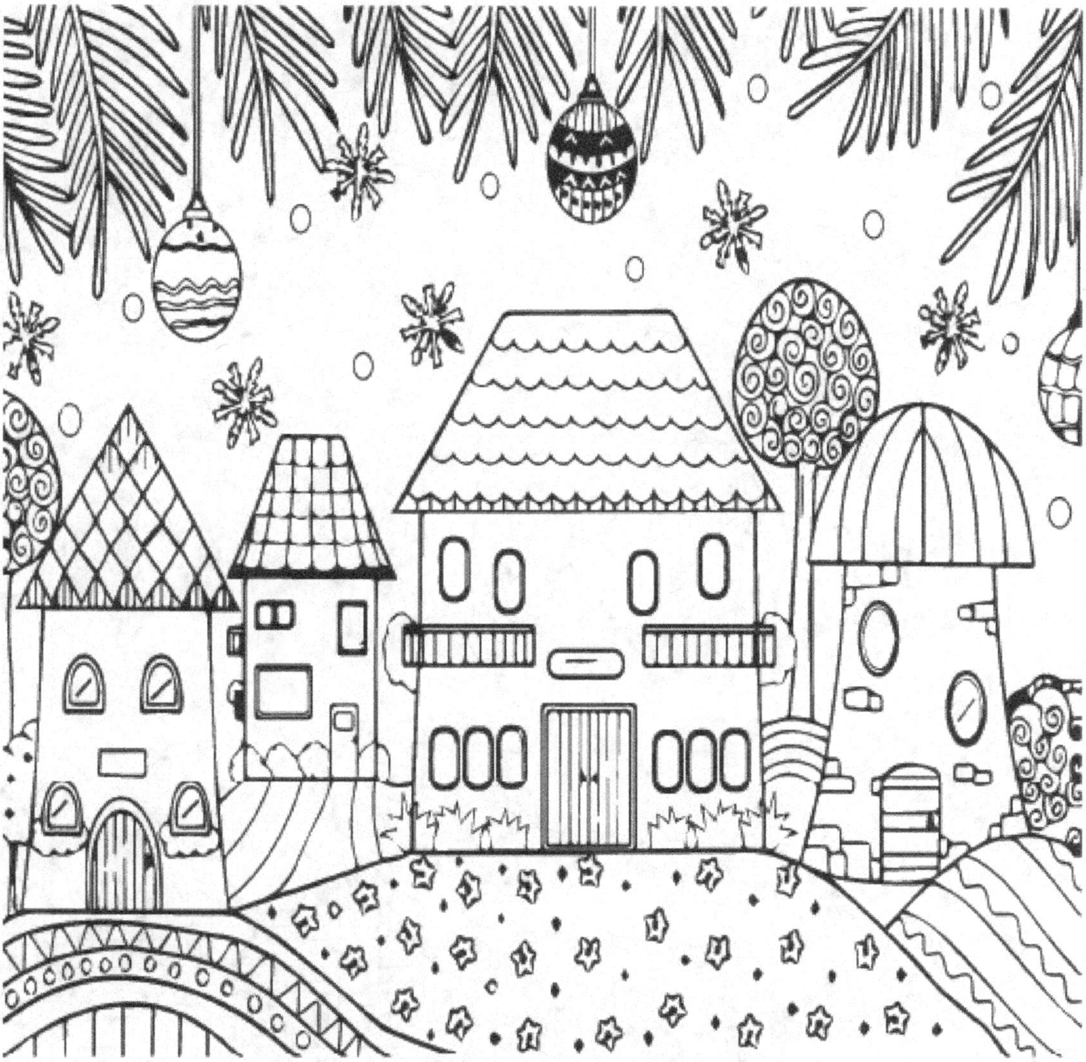

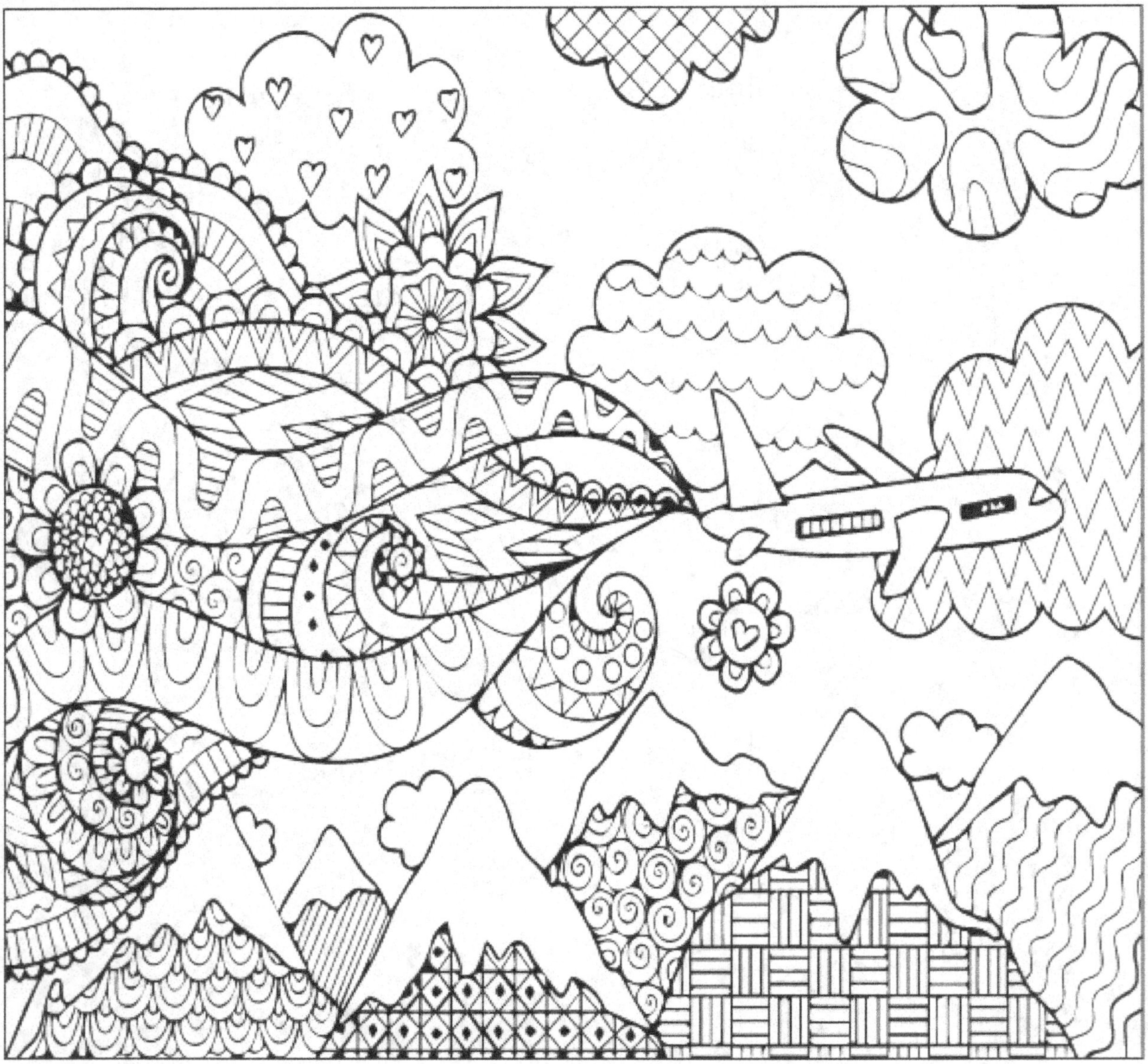

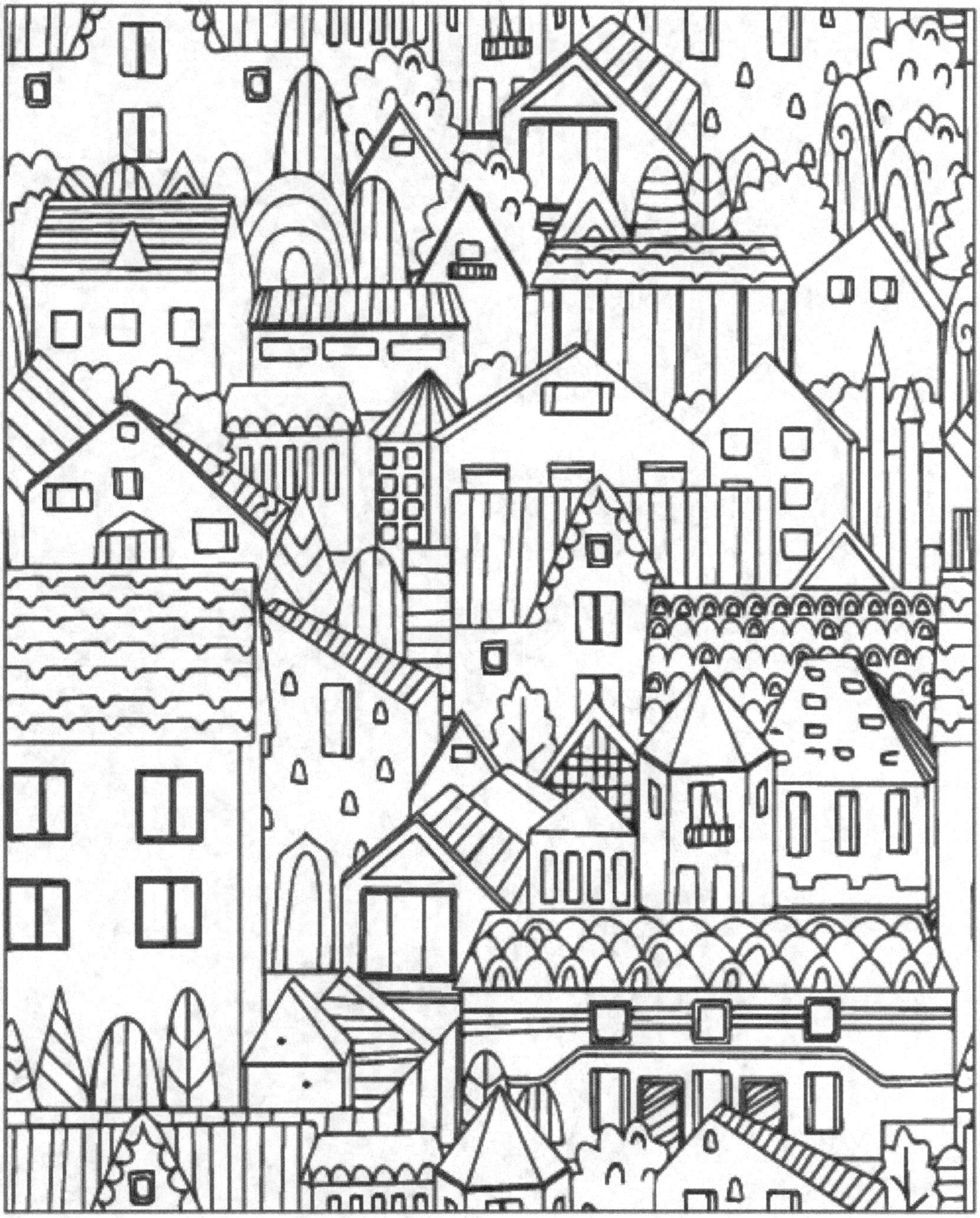

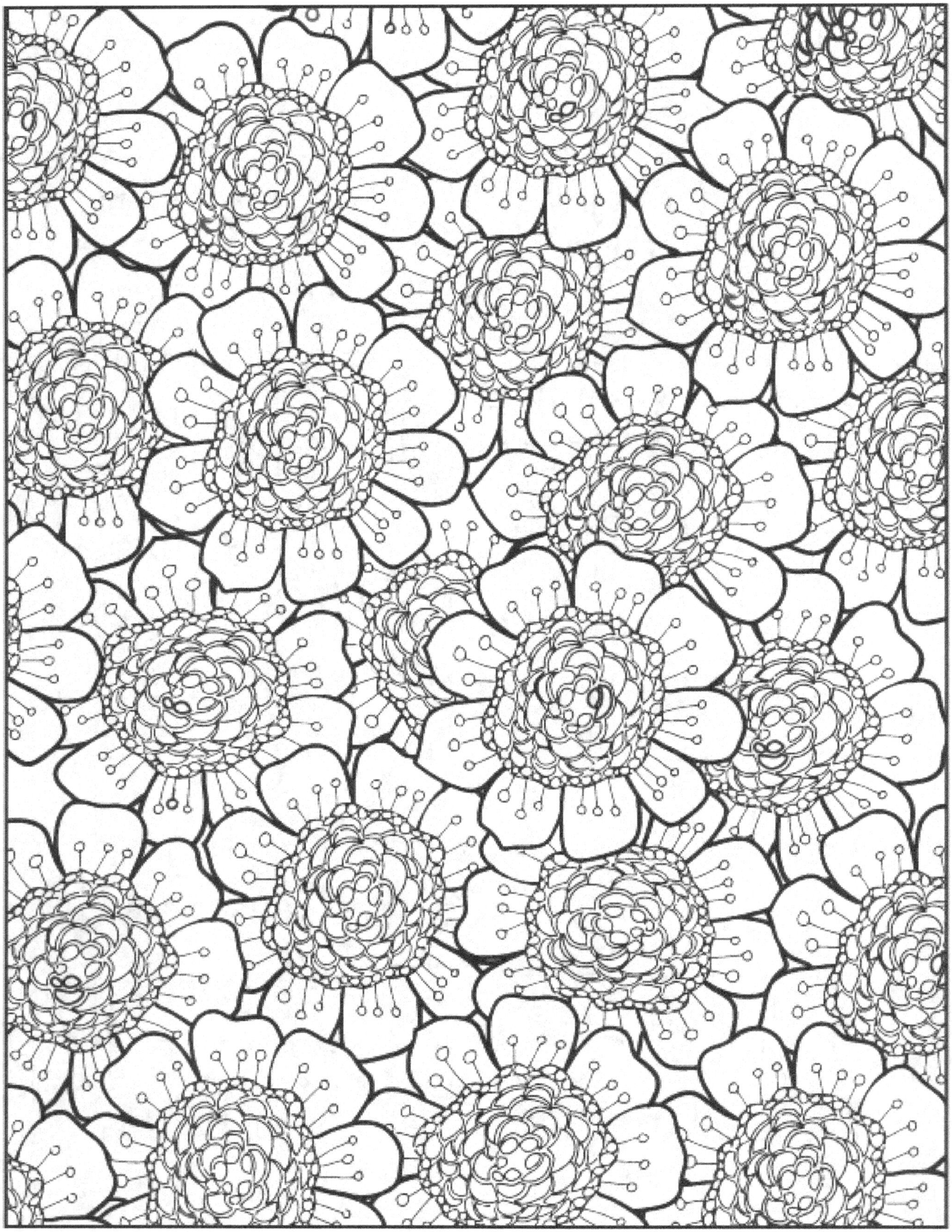

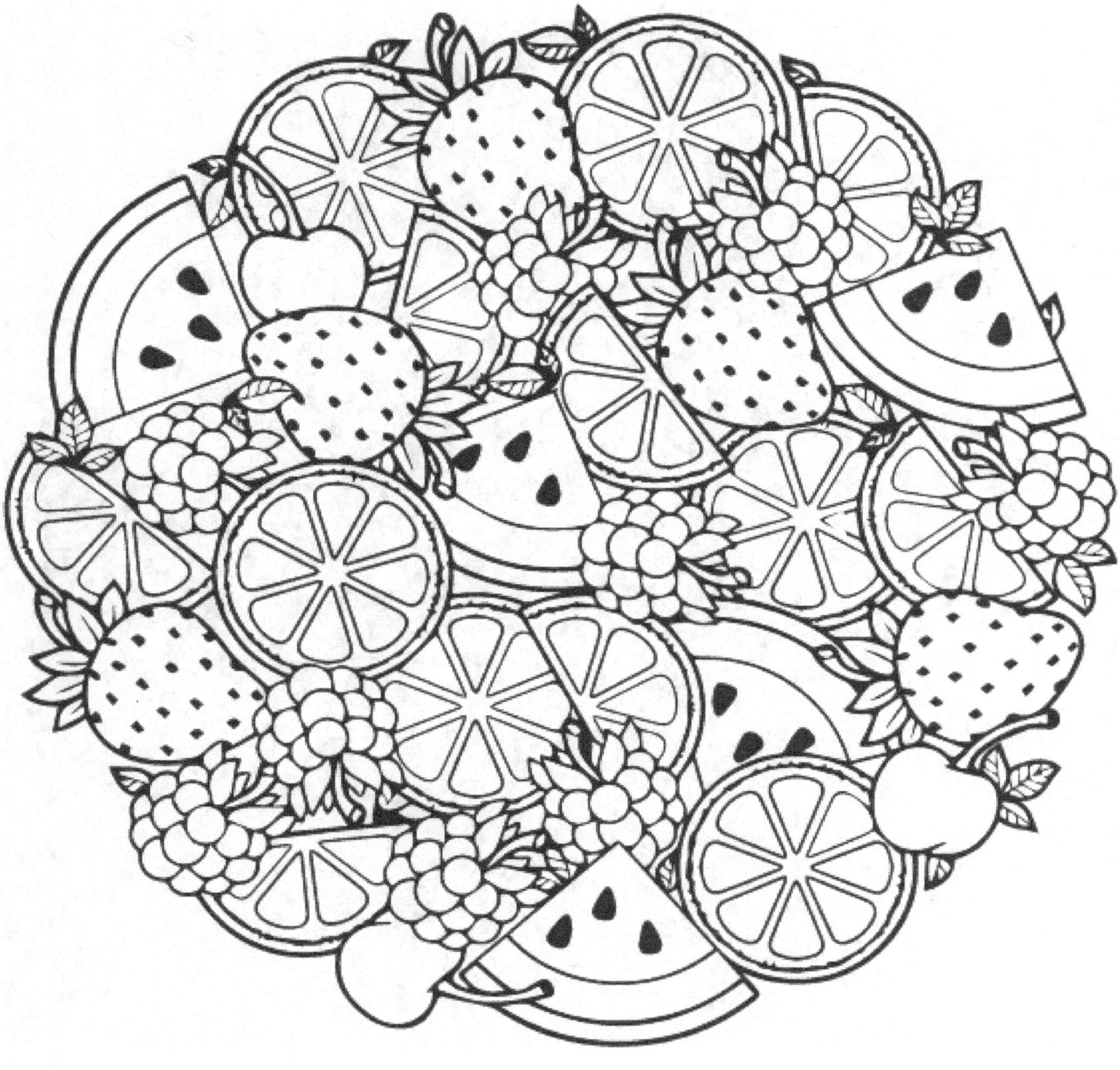

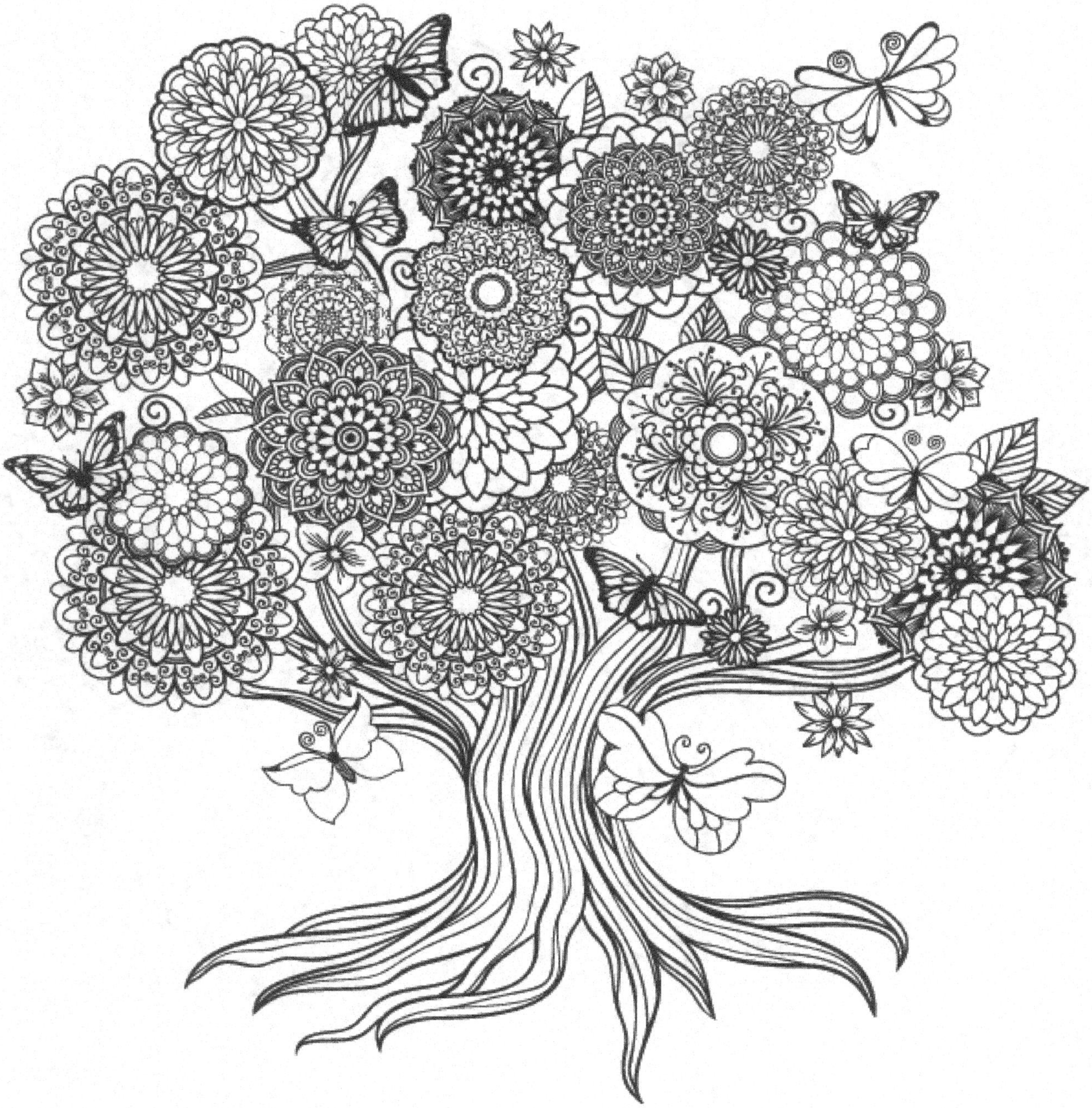

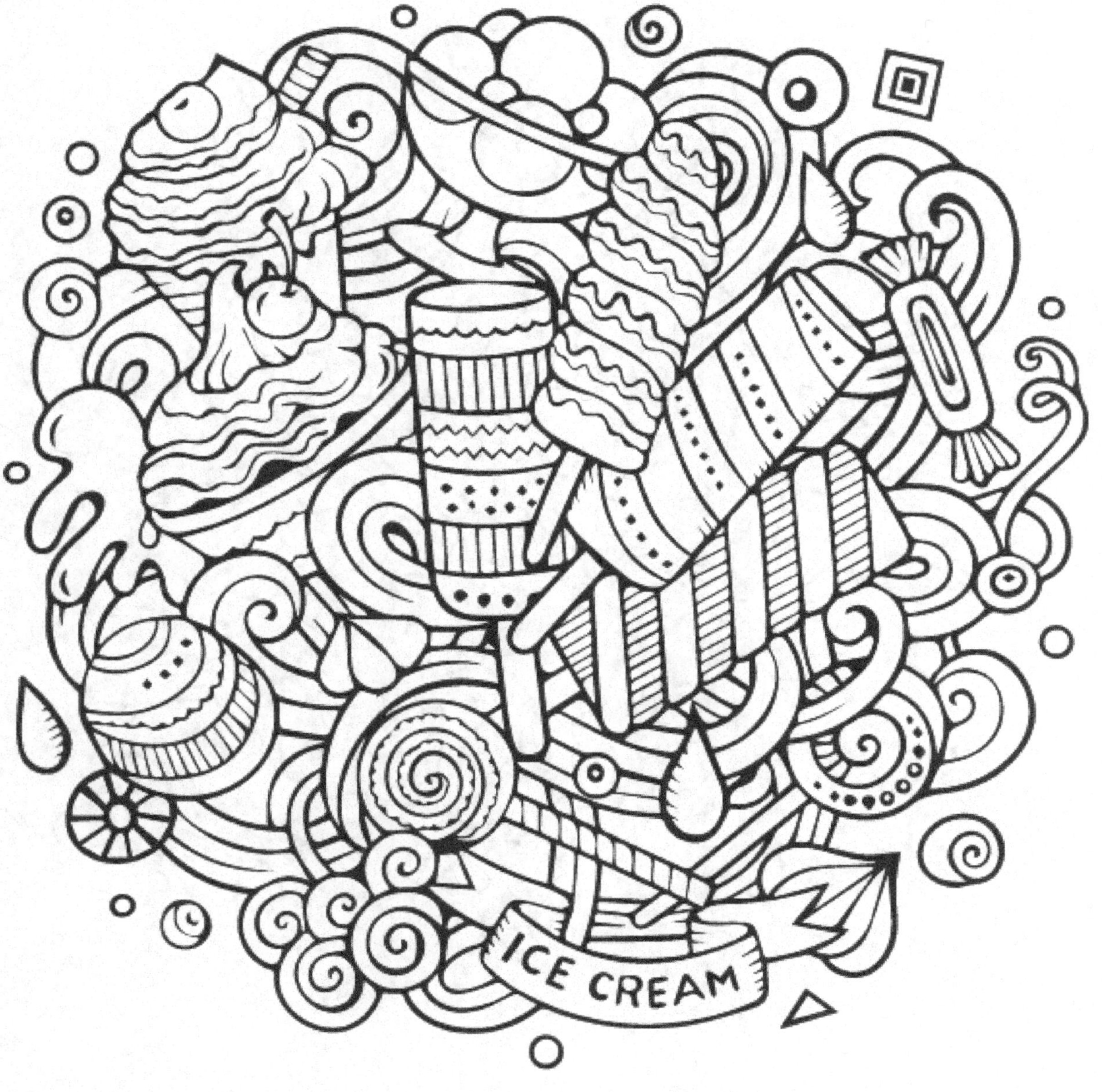
ICE CREAM

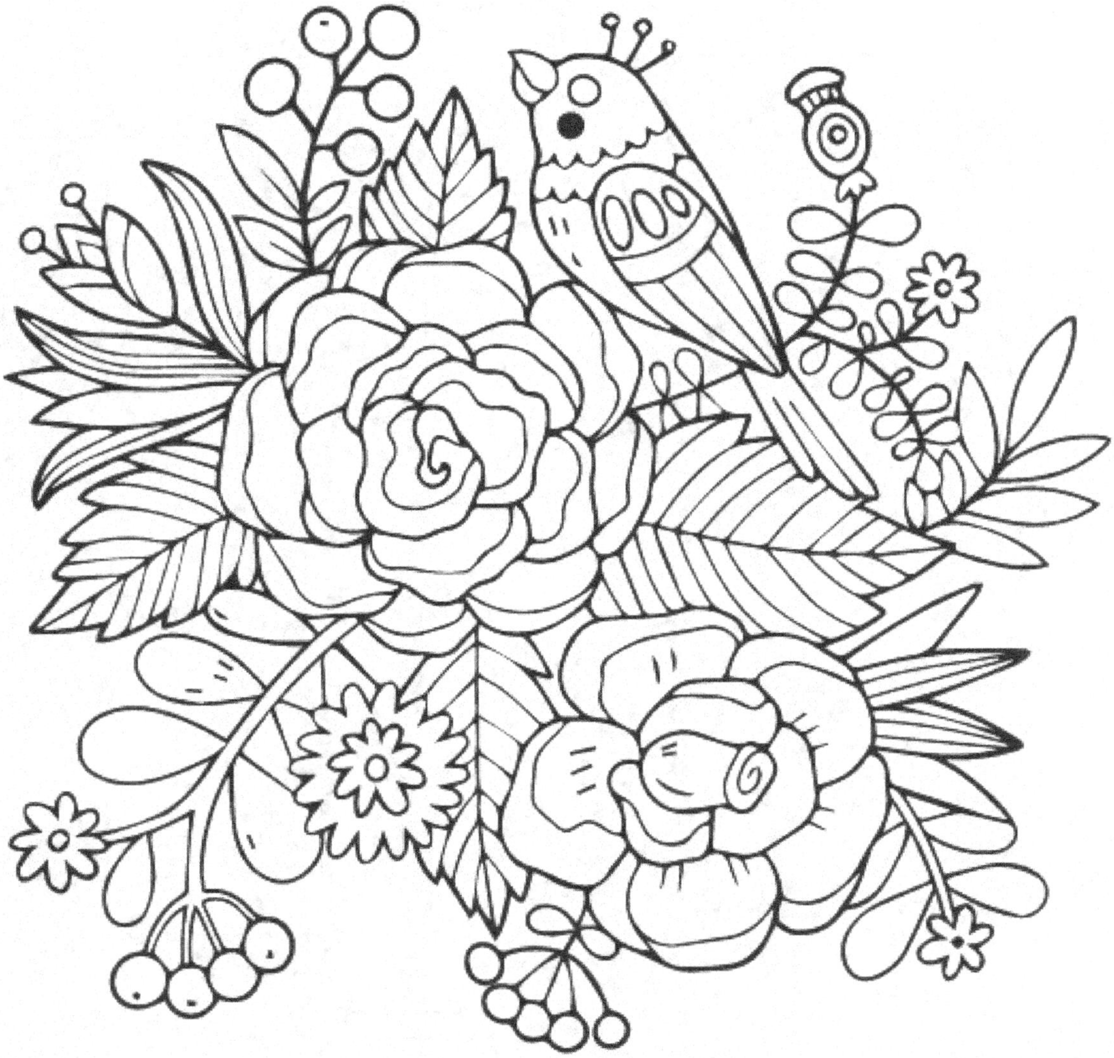

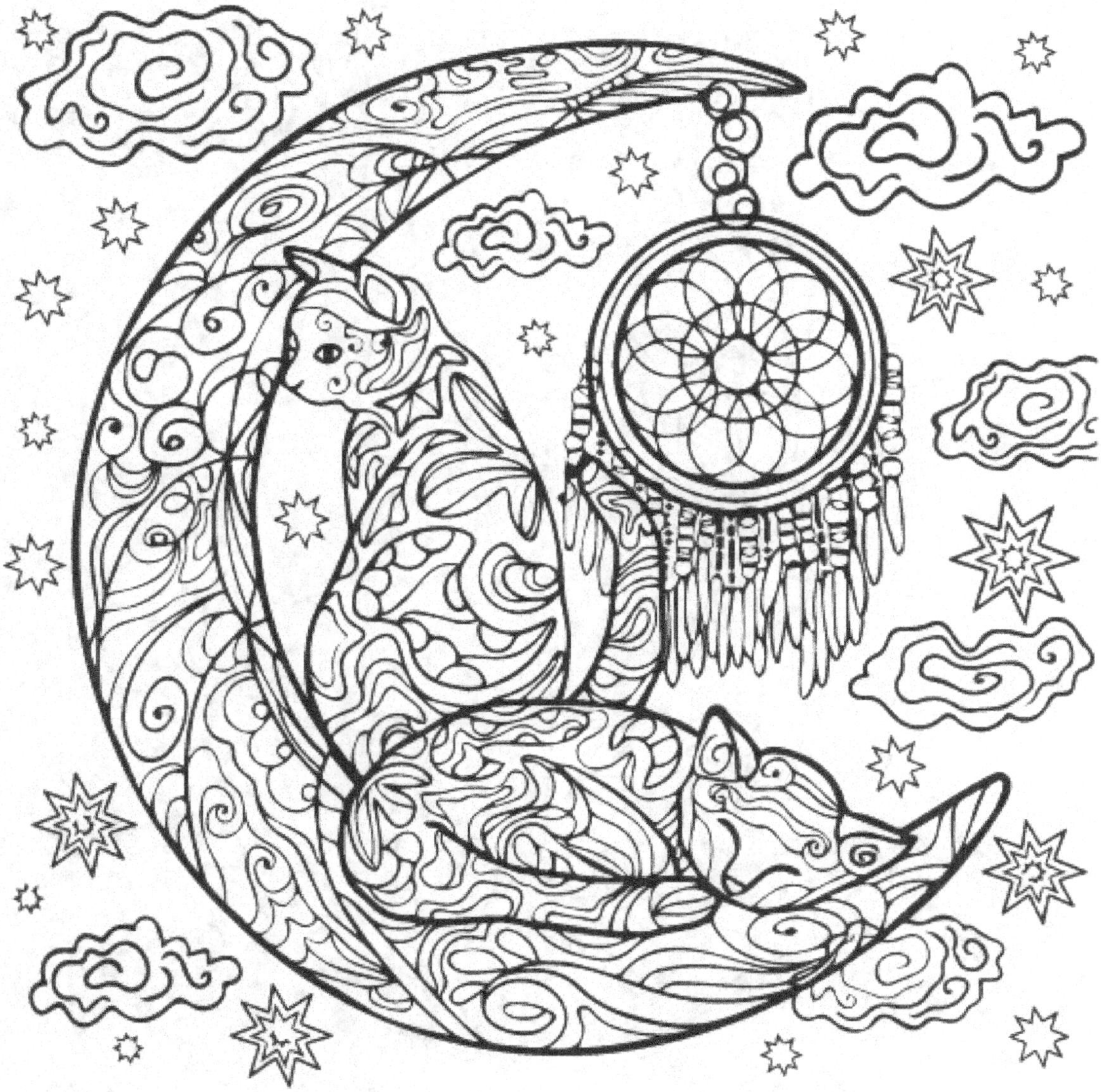

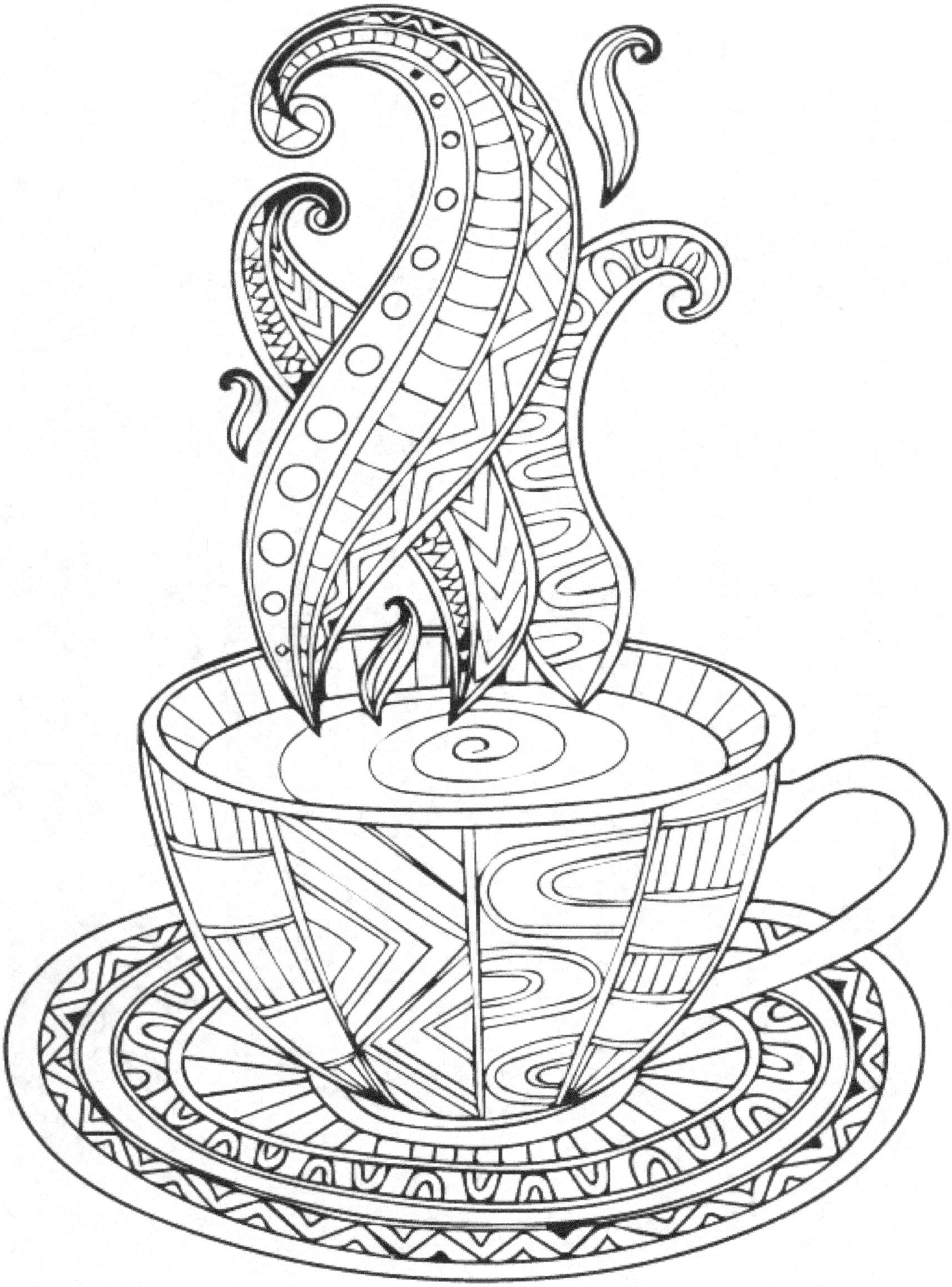

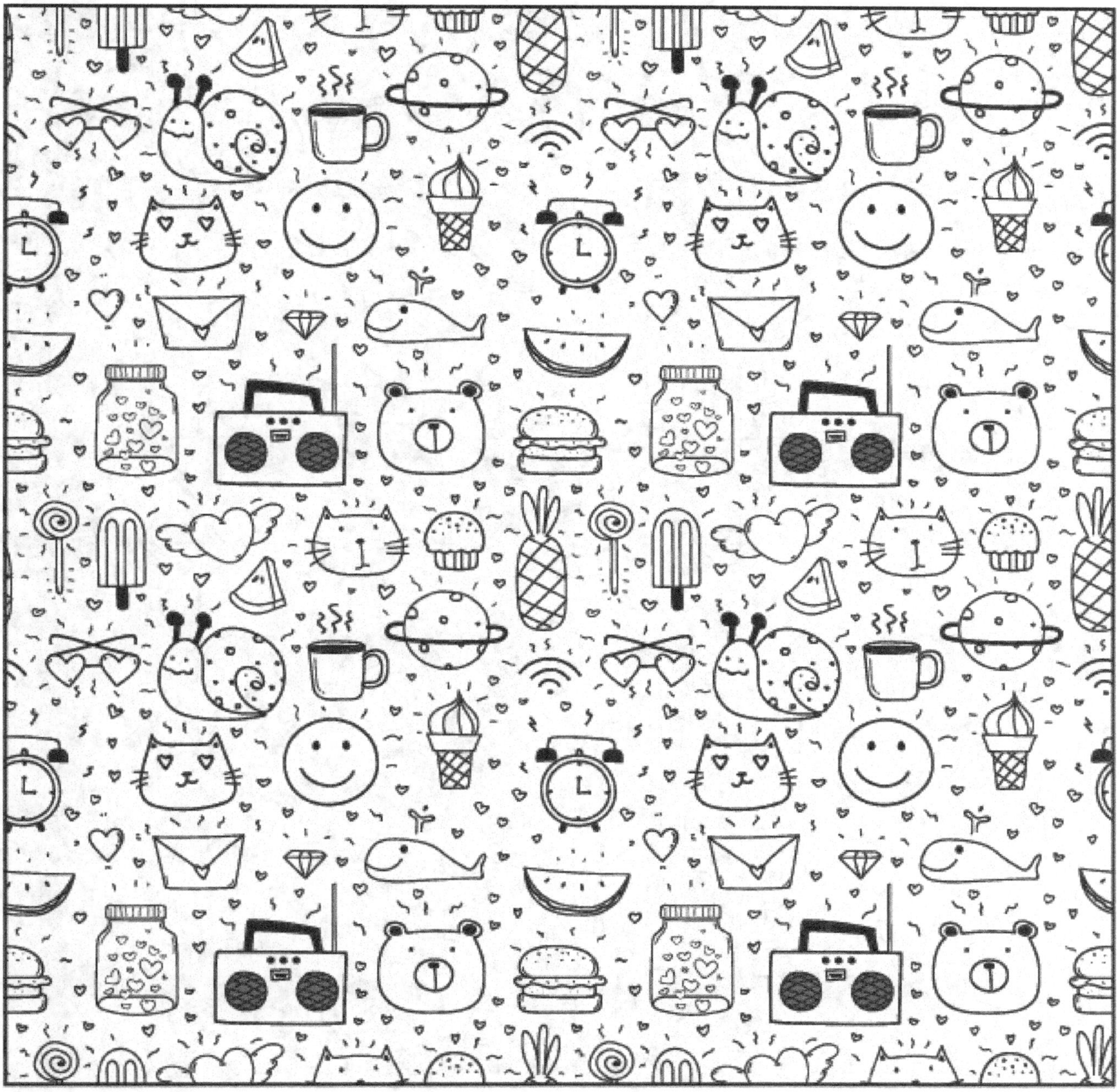

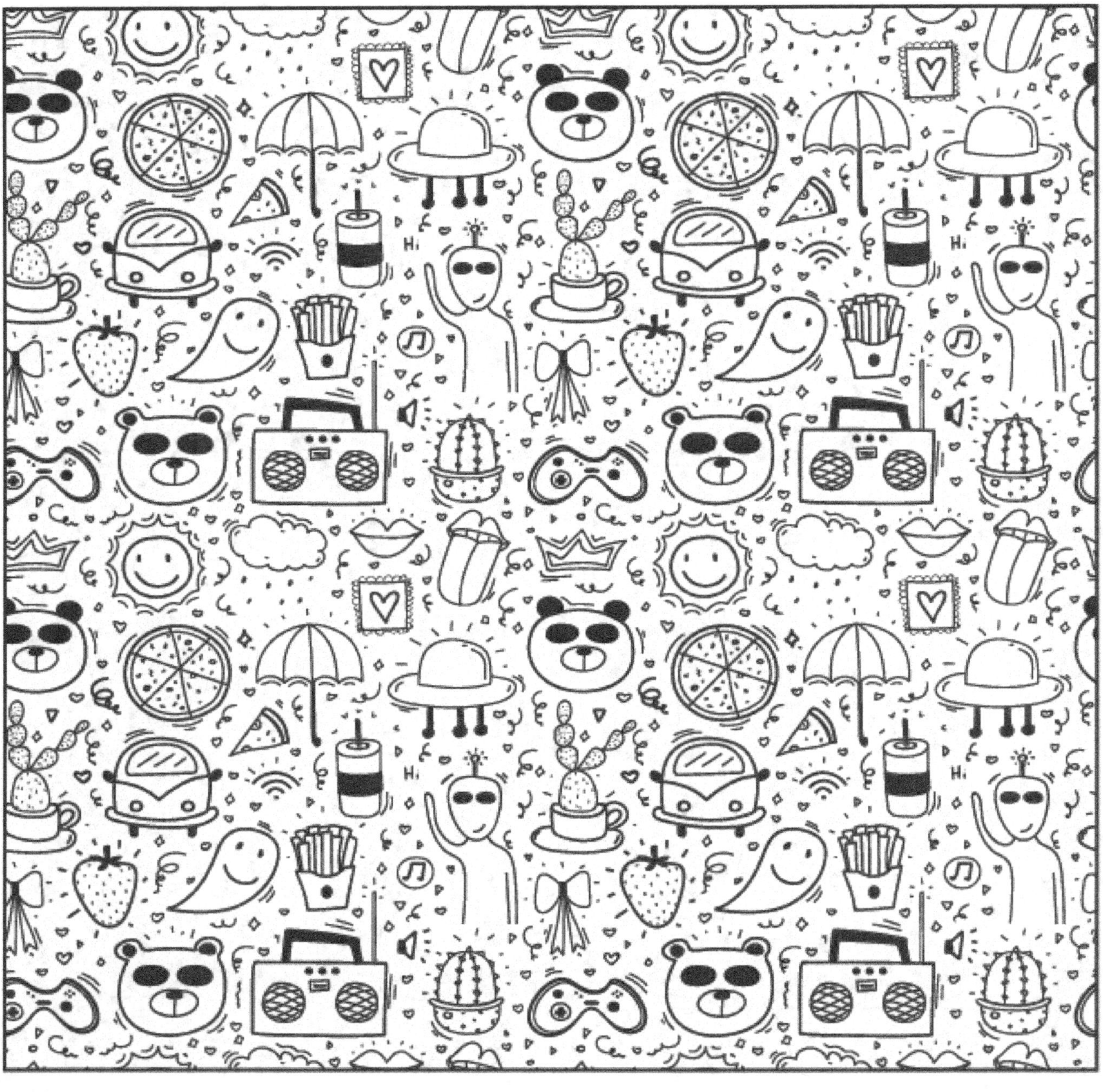
Hi

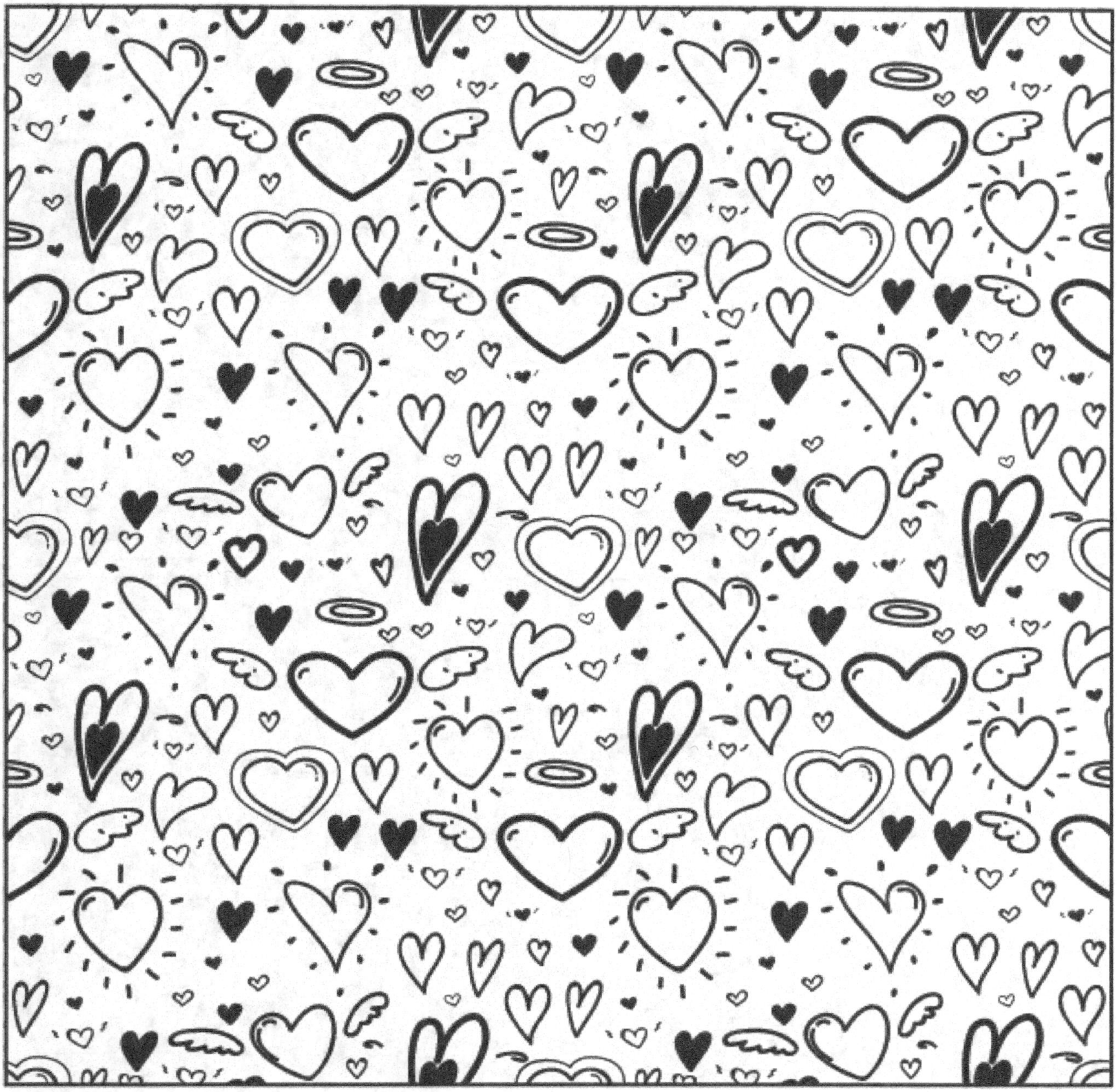

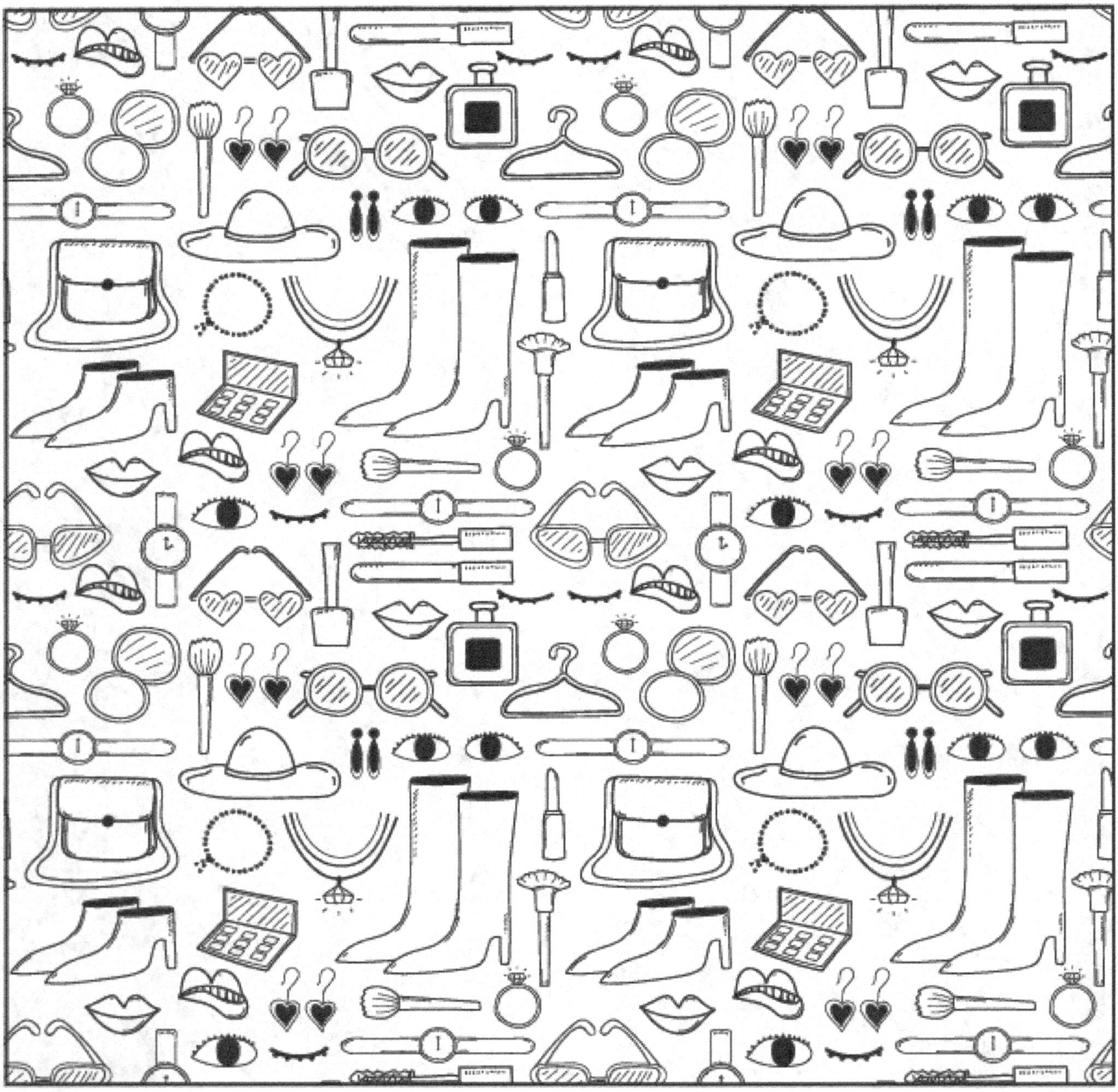

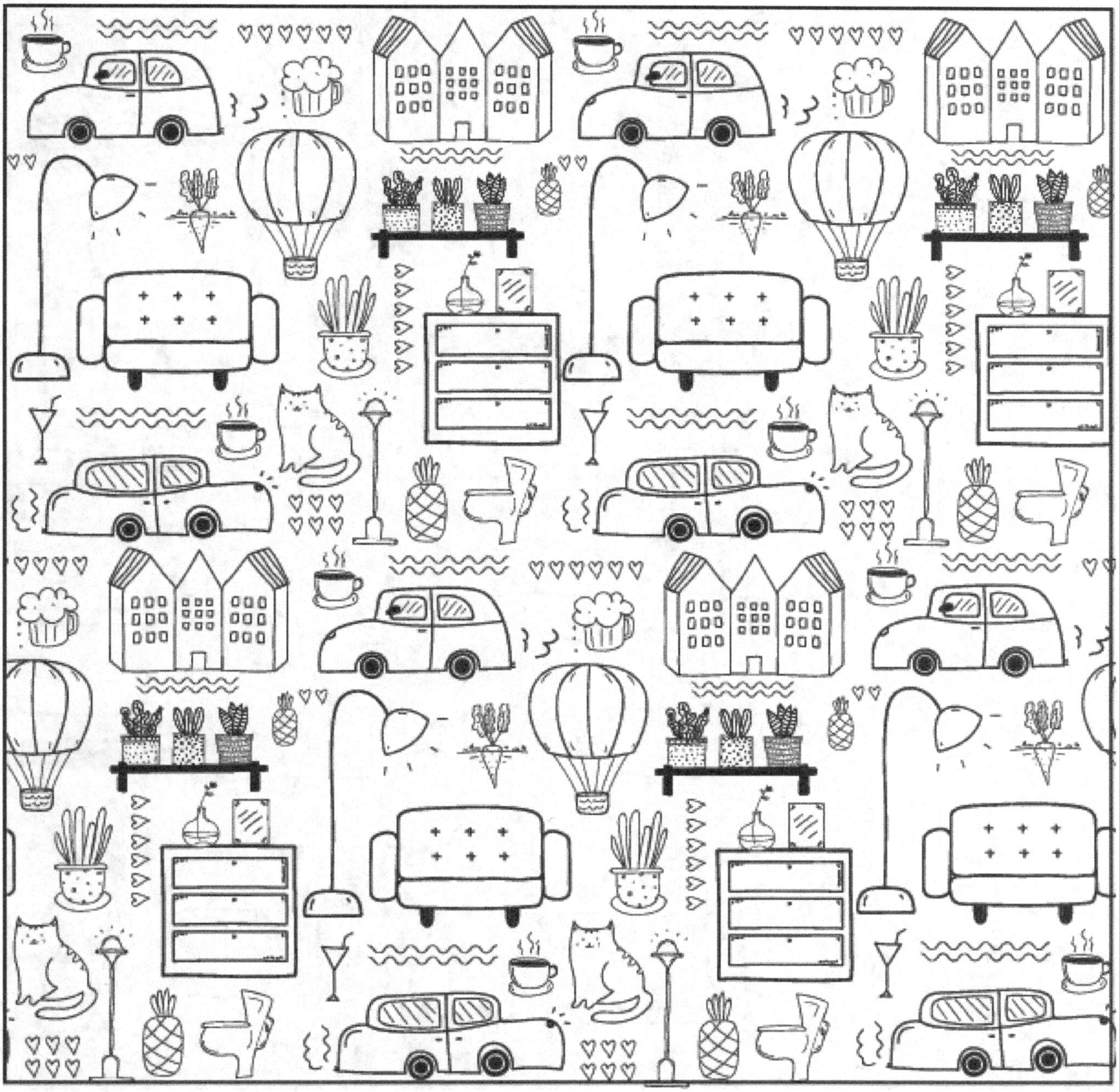

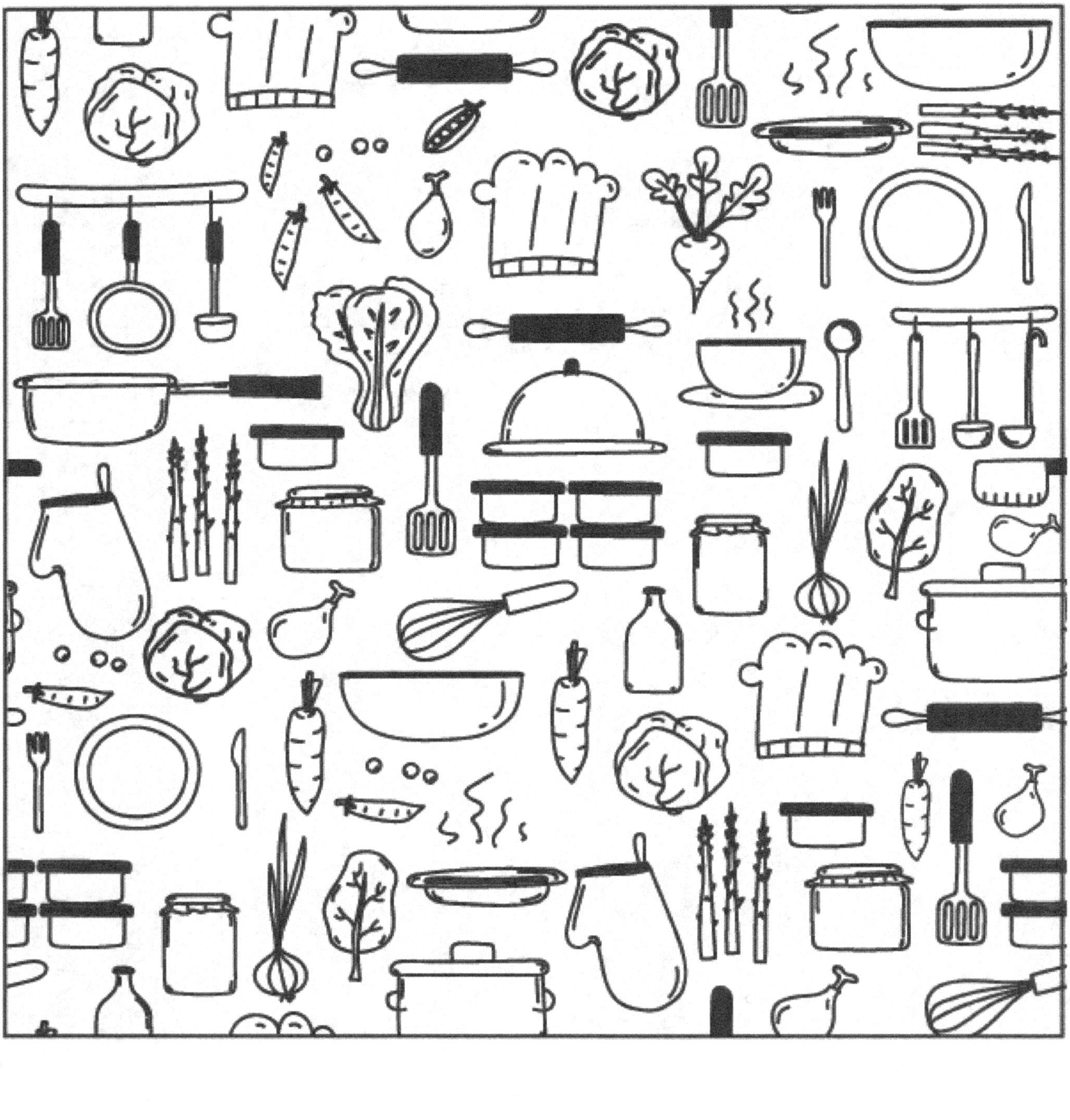

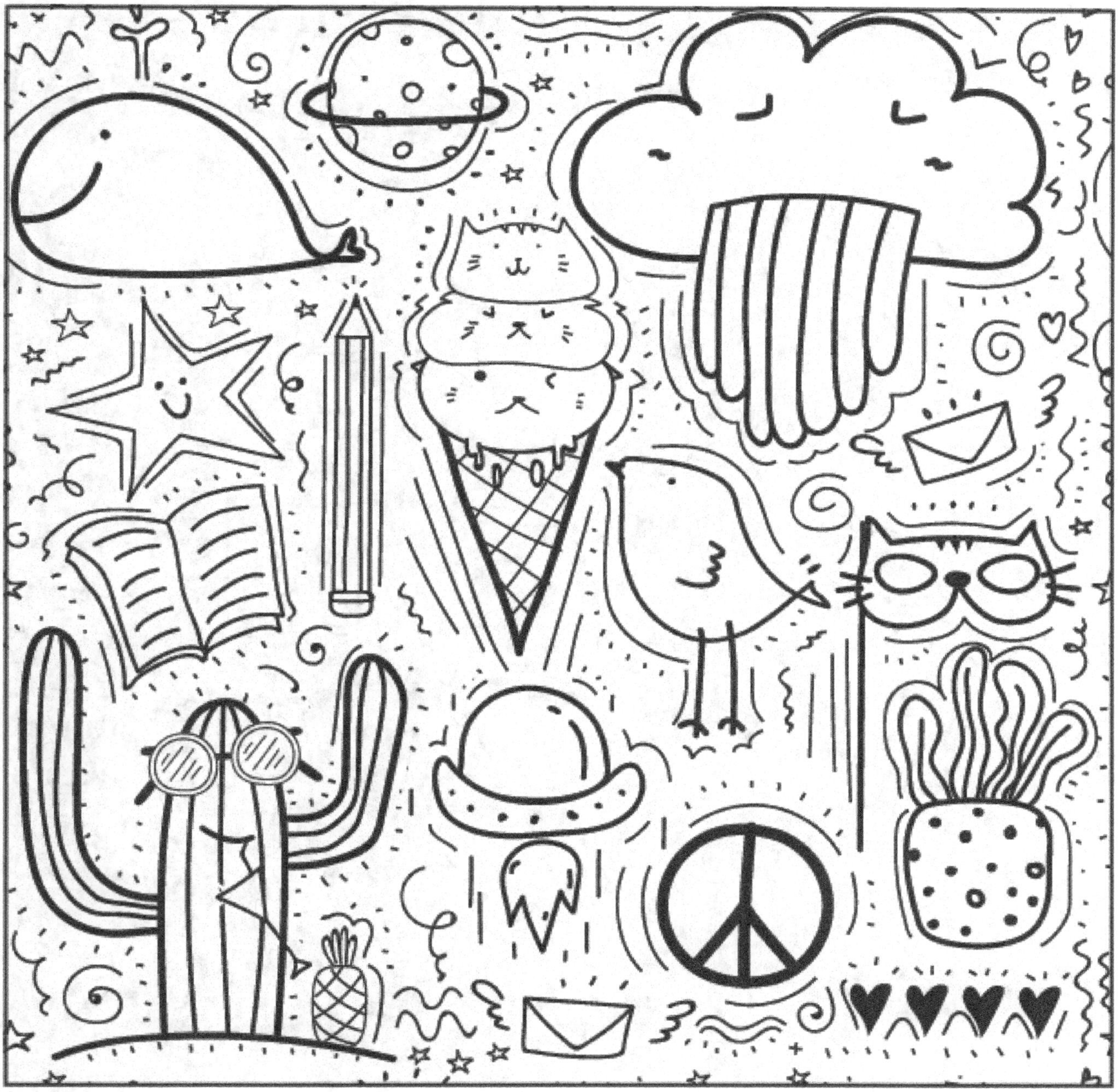

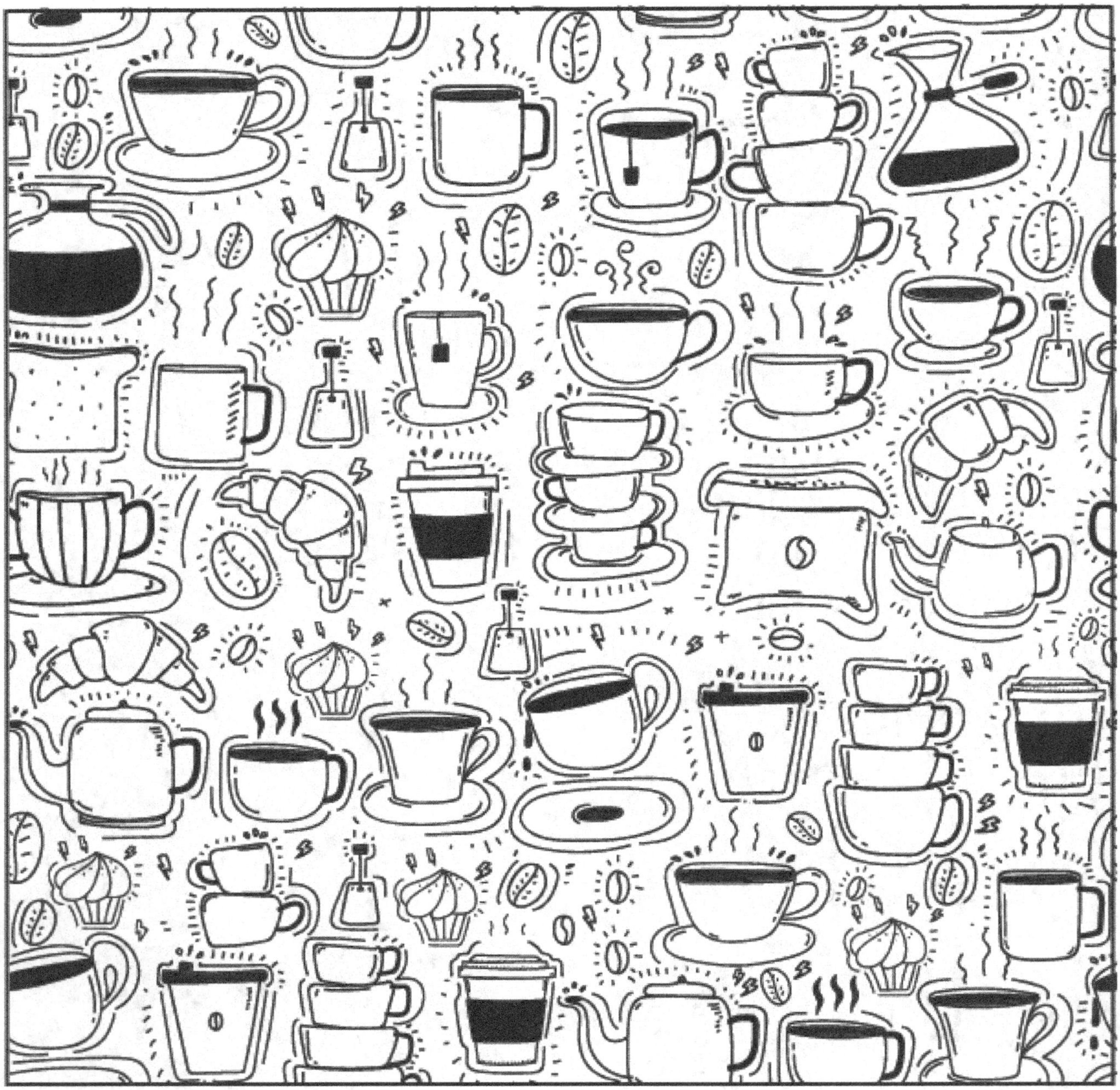

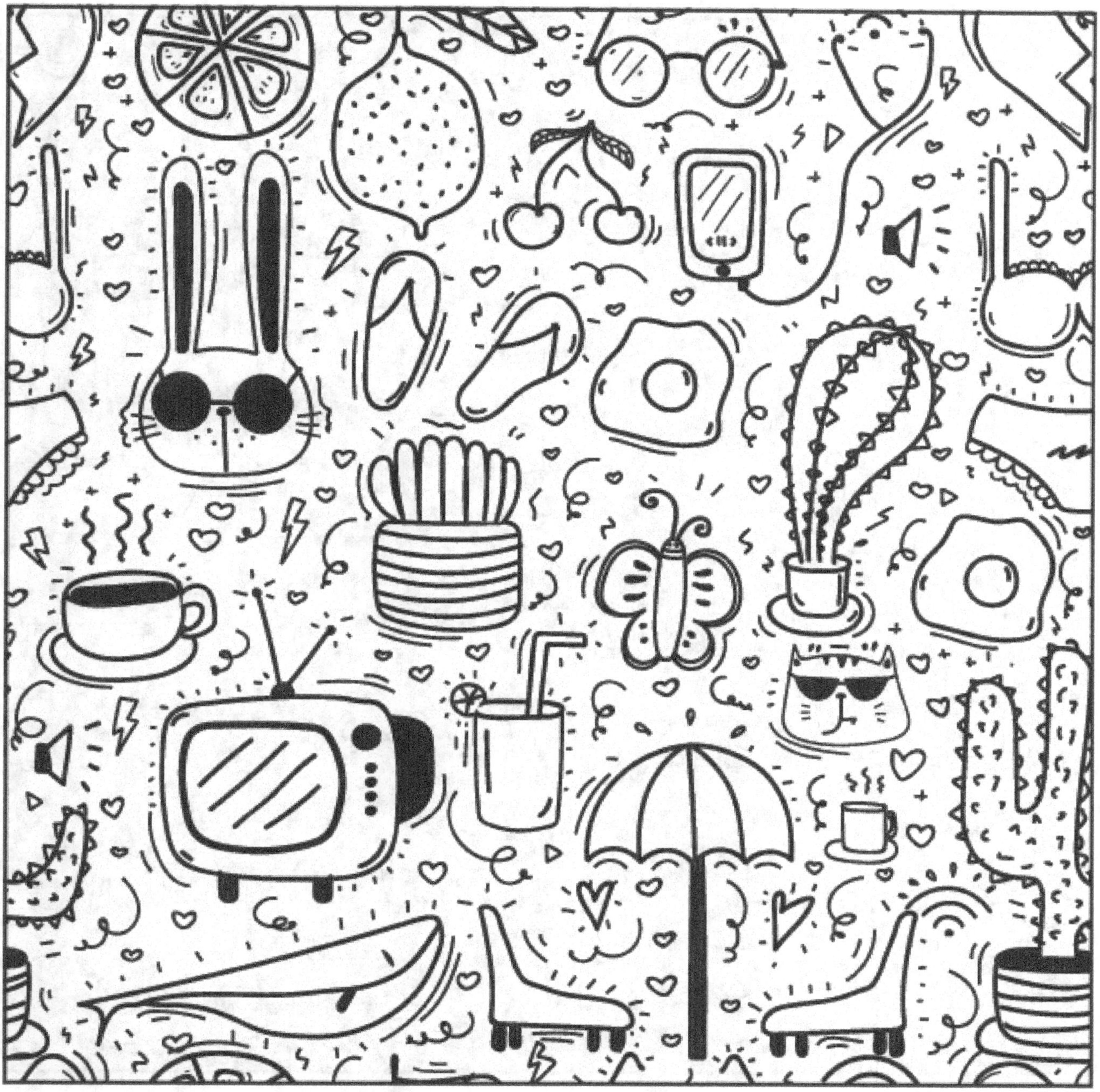

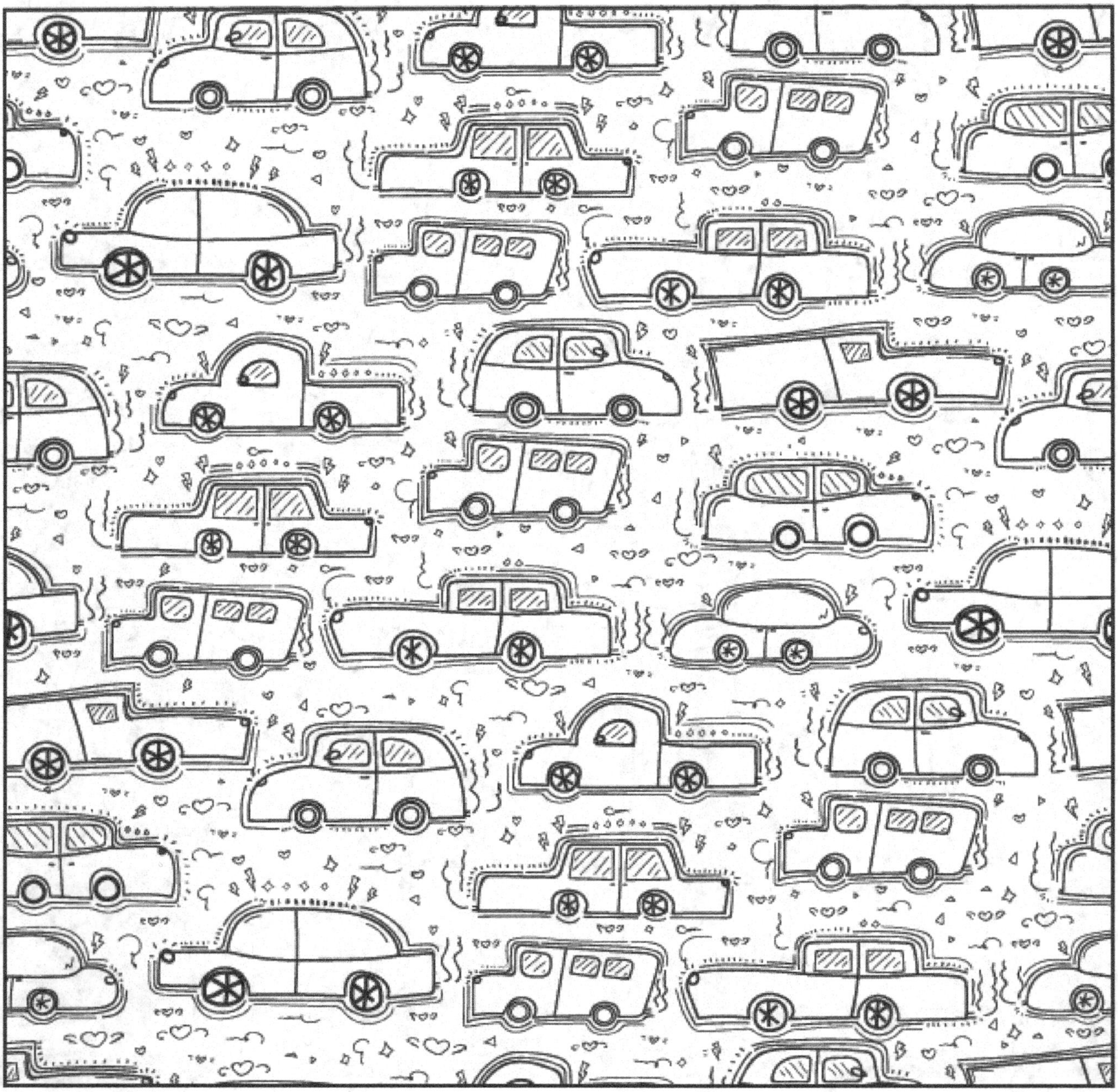

www.ingramcontent.com/pod-product-compliance
Lightning Source LLC
Chambersburg PA
CBHW080952220526
45465CB00008BA/3251
9798663567022